To: Mrs. Bobbie Milner
Thanks —
"The difference is made." you.
Best Wishes
Lonnie J. Edwards Sr.
4/26/02

A TEACHER'S TOUCH
Reaching Beyond Boundaries

**The
Lonnie Johnson Edwards
and
Nancy Johnson Miller
Story**

1stBooks rev. 6/14/01

TABLE OF CONTENTS

PREFACE

The year was 1971. Nancy Johnson met Lonnie Edwards.

For Nancy, a white fifth-grade student, the limitations were physical and emotional. Nubs in the place of fingers hindered activities, lowered self-confidence, and made her the object of ridicule by classmates.

For Lonnie Edwards, a first-year Physical Education teacher, the limitations were social. Unrealistic expectations for a novice teacher and a curriculum that didn't allow much creativity added to the challenges presented by being the first black male teacher in a predominately white school in the South.

Though differentiated by age, race, gender, and roles, Lonnie and Nancy possessed the same spirit and courage.

While Lonnie demonstrated a square dancing maneuver with Nancy, requiring their hands to touch, a life-changing interaction occurred. "Mr. Edwards" seized the opportunity to teach all of his students not to be afraid of limits imposed by physical or social stigmas. He taught them to reach beyond the boundaries.

More than twenty-five years later, Nancy Johnson Miller and Dr. Lonnie Edwards prove how far reaching a teacher's touch can extend.

DEDICATION

This book, <u>A Teacher's Touch: Reaching Beyond Boundaries,</u> is dedicated to:

- All teachers, for their committed service to educate all children

- The DeKalb County Board of Education, for offering me employment opportunities

- Wilburn Adams, former Associate Superintendent, for recruiting me

- Diane Carpenter, Alice Ann Hamilton, Eugene Thompson, and Narvie Harris, for their unswerving support of me during my early years of employment

- Hooper Alexander Elementary School's faculty, staff, administrators, 1971-1974 student body, and its surrounding community, for providing me with some of my greatest educational challenges as well as with some of my most unforgettable memories

- Nancy Johnson Miller, one of my former fifth-grade students, for publicly expressing gratitude to me for "making the greatest impact" on her life

- Cynthia Dorsey Edwards, my wife, for not only reading and editing my book, but also for her words of encouragement, loyal assistance, and dedication in "shepherding" this book from my pen to the printing press

- A host of family, friends, supporters, and well-wishers who encouraged me to write this book to highlight the importance of classroom teachers

ACKNOWLEDGEMENTS

A special "Thank You" is sent to:

- Sally Jessy Raphael, for selecting the Lonnie Edwards/Nancy Miller story to air on her show

- Doug Cumming, writer for the Atlanta Journal Constitution, for sharing this story in the print media, including submitting it to the Readers' Digest

- Readers' Digest, for featuring this story in their September 1997 issue, under "Heroes for Today"

- A host of local newspapers, for sharing this story with their readers and for providing continuing coverage on the Edwards-Miller Foundation for Physical Disabilities, Inc. (The Champion, Common Ground, The DeKalb Neighbor, The African Quest, Crossroads, The Decatur-DeKalb News/Era, Punto Hispano, and the Atlanta Journal Constitution)

- WXIA-TV/Channel 11-Alive, WAGA Fox5-TV, WSB-TV/Channel 2, and WGCL-TV/Channel 46 in Atlanta, GA, for coverage of this story and follow-up stories

- Archbishop Earl Paulk and the Cathedral of the Holy Spirit (Chapel Hill Harvester Church), my church, for commendations, support and encouragement

- Pastor James Powers, my personal pastor, Cathedral of the Holy Spirit, for his advice and counsel

- Dr. Joyce Giger, Diane Harvey, Garry McGiboney, Steen Miles, Billie Schwartz, and Charlotte Lemons for investing their time in reading and editing as well as in providing assistance in the packaging of **A Teacher's Touch**

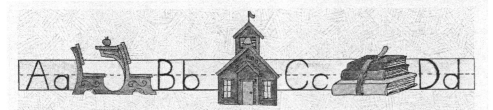

LONNIE

By
Nancy Johnson Miller

I WAS A SMALL CHILD OF EARLY YEARS
AND A STUDENT OF YOURS
WHO HOLDS YOU DEAR.

YOU TAUGHT ME TO HOLD MY HEAD UP HIGH
IT WAS YOU WHO MADE ME BELIEVE
THAT I COULD FLY.

HAVING KNOWN YOU ALWAYS
MADE ME FEEL BETTER
NO MATTER THE STORMS
THAT I HAD TO WEATHER.

YOUR DEDICATION MADE ME THE LADY I AM TODAY
I ONLY HOPE THAT I CAN GIVE BACK YOUR LOVE IN
SOME SPECIAL WAY.

YOUR WORDS OF WISDOM I CAN STILL HEAR
AND BECAUSE OF THIS
IN MY HEART
I WILL ALWAYS HOLD YOU DEAR.

FOREWORD

A Teacher's Touch is a book that should be read by everyone, especially those in the field of education. I truly enjoyed every line — every page. It flowed like a quiet river. I couldn't put it down. I laughed, and I cried; frequently, rereading pages through my tears. It so captivated my attention that I read it from cover to cover in one sitting.

If you're not an educator, you will still be encouraged by the sincere interest in a student shown by her teacher. You'll be inspired by the spunk of a physically challenged child and touched by seeing the interdependence of black and white individuals — reaching beyond the color line. You'll also be provided a first-hand look into what went on in the mind of a neophyte teacher.

If you are an educator, reading about the author's adventures in the classroom will invoke memories of your beginnings in the field of education. However, the author, Lonnie Edwards, was not quite prepared for the reception he received from the principal, the faculty, and many of the parents. Courses in education did not prepare him for the racist attitudes and behaviors that greeted him as he entered the teaching profession.

Lonnie faced many barriers that were designed to discourage him from teaching — initially, an oversized schedule of classes, which could not be handled effectively, under any circumstance, by one teacher; isolation by staff members; cold stares from parents; and more. As one might expect, many of these experiences caused him to question whether teaching was the right career choice for him. But, he *stayed the course.*

Academically, Lonnie knew that he was prepared to go into the classroom to train young minds assigned to his care. However, it was difficult for him to comprehend what all of the contrived barriers had to do with his teaching boys and girls.

Lonnie's experiences bring to mind a story I was once told: A mother stated to her daughter who was in a similar situation, "If they hate you because you are dirty, you can bathe. If they hate you because you are ignorant, you can become educated. But, if they hate you because you are black, tell them to have a talk with God."

The negative race-based experiences taught Lonnie humility, perseverance, determination, and the ability to endure. Never once did he retaliate or try to get even.   Instead, he used many avenues and techniques to share love, understanding, hope, and faith. He influenced a change in attitudes and brought humility to those whose minds were enslaved by making judgments based on the color of one's skin.

Mr. Edwards has gone on to become *Dr.* Edwards now. He has progressed from being a teacher to becoming a senior administrator in the DeKalb School System. Throughout his career, he has maintained a sincere focus on children and has consistently been an advocate for those who need help the most. His touch has made a difference in many lives.

I believe that you will thoroughly enjoy reading this book. It will make you think a little deeper and become a little more thankful. Most of all, it may help you renew your focus on your purpose in life so that you, too, can contribute to making the world a better place. As the adage says, "Service is the rent we pay for the space we occupy."

Narvie J. Harris, Retired Educator
DeKalb County, Georgia

Mrs. Narvie Harris was one of the first six African-American Jeanes[1] Supervisors employed by the DeKalb County School System during 1944. She established a reputation of excellence and high expectations as she progressed through the administrative ranks. As a result, without officially achieving the rank, she became known throughout the school district as "the Black Superintendent." Although Mrs. Harris retired in 1983, she is still active in many community organizations and is very influential in the educational community. In fact, in 1999, one of the new elementary schools built in DeKalb County was named in her honor.

[1] *Jeanes Supervisors were African-American men and women called upon to raise the education sight for "blacks" -- especially during the days of segregation. They were named "Jeanes Supervisors" in honor of Anna T. Jeannes, a white philanthropist and humanitarian, who donated funds to educate black boys and girls in the South.*

1

The Ultimate Surprise

The morning of September 17, 1996 began as a normal day. I woke up around 5:00 a.m. and silently prayed to God, thanking Him for another day. I lay in the bed for a while longer, assessing the previous day's activities, contemplating my plans for the day, and waiting for just a glimmer of the sun to come up.

Thinking of my schedule, I decided to get my daily exercise in the morning because I had a long day planned. While preparing for my run, I thought of all the plans I had made to surprise my wife, Cynthia, on her birthday that was only a week away, September 24th. The biggest surprise I had planned was flying her best friend from Chicago to visit with us in Atlanta for a few days. (Little did I know that the ultimate surprise was yet to come!)

After completing a two-mile run, along with doing other calisthenics, I showered, shaved and left for work. I ate my breakfast on the run.

My first stop was at a meeting with a group of community leaders concerning a constitutional amendment for a one-cent sales tax, which would be on the ballot on November 5, 1996.

I reached my office around mid-morning, greeted my staff and requested my urgent messages or phone calls. My secretary, Ms. Billie Schwartz, passed me a message from the Sally Jessy Raphael Show with numbers to call. There was an out-of-state number, along with an 800 number. Taking the message, I laughed, thanked her for it and requested the others.

Ms. Sara Neeley, a Community Liaison Specialist on my staff, started chattering — "Dr. E, what have you gotten into now?" I returned the chatter by saying, "I don't know." Somewhat going along with what I thought was probably a prank they had gotten together to play on me, I took a casual position and said, "Thank you, ladies, for the message. I will call the Sally Show later on today." Then, Billie said it was a legitimate call and that they wanted me to return the call that morning.

Ninety-nine times out of a hundred, if Billie reports something, it is true. But, I thought that this time, the group was influencing her. Her next statement was, "Dr. Edwards, would I mislead you?" Looking at her, I still wasn't sure, but I thought, "Maybe it is a legitimate call." So, I went to my desk to make the call. However, when Ms. Neeley followed me into my office to make sure that I called The Sally Show, I became suspicious again. I was sure that they were up to mischief.

Nevertheless, with their continued encouragement, I dialed one of the numbers and, sure enough, the operator answered by saying that I had reached the Sally Jessy Raphael Show. I told the operator that my name was Lonnie Edwards from Atlanta, Georgia and asked to speak with Sally Jessy Raphael. When I was transferred, the voice on the other end of the line said, "Lonnie Edwards, we have been trying to track you down." I said, "Is that so?" The voice said, "Yes, my name is Sally, the host of the Sally Jessy Raphael Show." I asked how I could help her. She said she would like to ask me a few questions. I was still thinking the ladies in the office were pulling off a prank, but I agreed to answer the questions. The dialogue went something like this:

"Do you know Nancy Miller?"
"No. Next question."
"Have you ever taught grade school?"
"Yes, twenty-three years ago."
"Do you know a disabled woman by the name of Nancy Miller?"

This time, I responded by saying that I had no idea who she was talking about and that I was sure she had the wrong Lonnie Edwards. (I had discovered about two years earlier that there were a lot of people named Lonnie Edwards.)

I then asked her a question, "Ma'am, how did you get my number?" She told me that a young white woman with a disability had written to the show and told them that I had made the greatest impact on her life. She said that she would forever be grateful and wanted to publicly thank me on the show. I responded by saying, "Ma'am, let me say for the last time that you have the wrong Lonnie Edwards because I don't know a Nancy Miller."

By that time, I was nearing the end of the conversation because each question was repetitive, "Have you taught grade school?" or "Do you know Nancy Miller?" Ms. Raphael asked me not to hang up; she could tell by my responses that I was running out of patience. I said I would not hang up on her, but I was just sure that she had the wrong Lonnie Edwards.

Then, she said she had one last question. I told her to go ahead and ask it. She asked, "Have you ever taught square dancing?" I responded, "Oh, my God, ma'am, yes, but that was twenty-plus years ago." Then, she asked again, "Do you remember a student by the name of Nancy Miller?" Square dancing triggered my memory, and I responded by saying, "If this is the same person, her name was Nancy, but not Miller. It was something else at the time. The Nancy I remember was a little white girl I met while teaching P.E. who had been born without a full set of fingers on either hand. If this is who I now think it is, I am really touched. I knew her by another name. I don't know a Nancy Miller, but if she is who I now think she is, I feel a little choked up."

I went on to tell Ms. Raphael that this had happened nearly twenty-five years before. She asked how old I was at that time. I told her that I was 48 years old; so, 25 years ago, I was 23. She told me that I was still just a baby. I laughed and told her that if she thought 48 was young, she could call me every day. She laughed and said she'd like to ask me a few more questions. She asked if I was African-American. I told her that I was. She said, "This is a phenomenal story. You were just a child yourself when this happened. Tell me more."

As I shared with Ms. Raphael about my involvement with Nancy, I thought about how far I had come, and the memories of my childhood as well as of that time — over twenty-five years ago — came back to life, as vividly as if they took place only yesterday.

2

The Transition -
From Mississippi to Georgia

I was born and reared on my maternal grandparents' farm, about 100 acres of land, in Shaw, Mississippi, a small rural city. This area of the state is also known as "the Delta." I was my parents' first-born and the oldest grandchild. My grandfather died when I was very young, and my grandmother, Abbie Johnson, was the epitome of the "grand matriarch" of the family. She was the glue that held the family together.

As a child, I worked on the family farm. I chopped and picked cotton, milked the cows, fed the hogs and chickens, and, as I grew older, drove the tractor. I had to miss school about 30 days in the Fall of every year due to the harvest time ... time to pick cotton. Each year, when I returned to school, I knew that I had gotten behind in some of the coursework. So, I would sit on the back row until I could begin to catch up with the other students. As I began to master the lesson, I would move up a row at a time until I was on the front row again. It wouldn't take me long. I was competitive and loved to learn.

When I graduated from high school, I first went to Coahoma Junior College, a predominately black two-year college in Clarksdale, Mississippi. Since I was considered an "outstanding" basketball player, I had been able to obtain an athletic scholarship to the school. I completed my education there on the Honor Roll, with a "B" grade point average. Several years later, I was later inducted into the Coahoma Junior College Basketball Hall of Fame.

After receiving my Associate's degree from Coahoma, I entered the University of Montevallo, a predominately white four-year college in Montevallo, Alabama. I was the first black male athlete to enroll in that institution. I was awarded an athletic scholarship to the college and was permitted to bring another student with me. I chose one of my Coahoma basketball pals, Hansell Gunn. I graduated from Montevallo on schedule and was awarded my degree "With Highest Honors." I was also later inducted into their Basketball Hall of Fame.

When I left the University of Montevallo in 1971, my sight was set on playing for a team in the National Basketball Association (NBA). I was invited to the Chicago Bulls Rookie Camp and hoped that I would end up one of the lucky ones to be selected for the pros. More than one hundred young men tried out for the team that year. I was selected to stay down to the last ten before I was cut. My birth date had been assigned a lottery number #51 in the military draft, and I was classified 1-A. It was during the Vietnam War. The coaches (and I) figured that it was only a matter of time before I would be inducted into the military. The Bulls couldn't start the season with me, knowing that they would probably lose me right away. Norm Van Lear was assigned to "my slot."

My best friend from college, Earnest Killum, had graduated a year before I did and had been selected to play for the Los Angeles Lakers. However, by the end of his first year, he had broken his ankle; this injury prematurely ended his career. So, when I was cut from the Bulls, we commiserated together and wondered what was next on our career agendas.

I went to Chicago, Illinois for the summer to live with my father and to work wherever I could. While there, Richard Wark, a Personnel Recruiter with the DeKalb County Board of Education, contacted me to come to work as a Physical Education teacher in the Georgia school system. Other representatives from the DeKalb School System had interviewed me during the Spring prior to my graduating from Montevallo University. During my discussion with Mr. Wark, I told him that my lottery number was #51 and that I might be going into the military soon. However, he encouraged me to start work with them anyway. Happy to have an opportunity to secure a stable job with benefits, I quickly accepted the offer to move to Georgia.

(Three months into the school year, I received my induction papers. I gave them to my Principal thinking that in a few weeks I would be on my way to the war. However, a few days later, I was notified that I had been given a six-month deferment. And, before the six months were up, joining the military became voluntary again. Within a year, I had other opportunities to play professional basketball, including an invitation to play in Australia. However, I appreciated DeKalb giving me an opportunity at a new career, so I declined to leave the teaching profession. Anyway, by then, I had become "hooked" on the kids.)

3

The Stage

In 1971, when I arrived in the city of Decatur, a suburb about 15 miles outside the city of Atlanta, I that found the tone in the community was one of resistance, anger and bitterness as black parents fought to keep the schools in their communities open, while white parents fought to the same end — to keep Blacks in their own community. Their motives, however, were slightly different. The white parents were more concerned with keeping Blacks away from their children than they were with the convenience of their attending schools near home.

DeKalb, one of the largest public school systems in the state of Georgia, was under a federal court order to dismantle segregated schools. Though viewed as a positive social change, this mandate evoked a rash of negative responses from parents, school system employees, students, the business community and others who simply decried the change. More accurately, people feared the results of this conversion. Fear of the unknown posed a greater threat to some than the possibility of what could actually occur. Some white families opted to move out of their communities to avoid integration (white flight). Black families resented being forced to send their children to schools where they were not wanted or welcomed. School officials, attorneys and staff frequently assessed their behaviors and decisions to ensure that they were not in violation of the mandate.

Needless to say, these changes created a tense environment for everyone who lived, worked or played within the boundaries of the DeKalb County School System. It certainly did for me as I embarked upon my teaching career.

4

Coming Aboard

When I accepted my first teaching position with the DeKalb County School System in August 1971, a number of communities were experiencing their first wave of racial transition. Such was the case in the Hooper Alexander Elementary School community to which I was assigned. This was not my first encounter with racial tension as I had recently graduated from the University of Montevallo (in Montevallo, Alabama), which was, as I said before, a predominately white college where I was one of only a few blacks to attend. There, I had experienced being the only black in many of my classes and one of only two living in my dormitory. Being teased, belittled, berated, ignored and the victim of sophomoric pranks by white classmates were as much a part of my college experience as academics. As I left Montevallo, I thought I was leaving behind the injustices. To my chagrin, it proved to be only basic training for my present assignment.

Hooper Alexander Elementary School's staff size was close to fifty; six of whom were black (four teachers, a food service worker and a janitor). I was the only black male teacher. The tension on the staff was just as thick as it was in the community. Black staff members were nervous about congregating together, fearing that others might accuse them of strategizing a protest. White teachers said only what was necessary to blacks so as not to be perceived as being too friendly or as too accepting of the transition.

My first battle was not with students or co-workers, but with the school Principal, Mr. David Christopher. When I met with him to get my schedule, I learned that he and the sixth- and seventh-grade teachers had met secretly the previous evening to plan my schedule and class locations. The schedule that they had devised for me would have posed a tremendous challenge to a veteran teacher and certainly proved to be a Herculean task for a novice!

My schedule included all the sixth- and seventh-grade classes the other teachers didn't want! I was assigned Biological and Physical Science, Health, and Math. These classes accounted for 49% of my schedule. The remaining

51% of the time, I was to coordinate and teach Physical Education (P.E.) for all students, grades kindergarten through seven. Looking at that schedule, I knew I was being programmed to fail, but I had to give it the old college try!

After leaving the Principal's office, I searched for my classroom and the Physical Education room. En route, I passed a white seventh-grade teacher who rudely turned her face toward the wall to avoid speaking to me. Seeing this, I thought, "The more exposure I have to the people in this school, the more I dislike it!" As I sat in my classroom, reviewing my schedule and reflecting on the attitudes and behaviors of the administrator and my co-workers, I made a decision—I had to leave! But then, I thought, "Maybe I should give the Principal another opportunity to modify my schedule before bailing out." So, I returned to Mr. Christopher's office for another chat.

When I entered the main office, the secretary bluntly asked what I wanted. I told her that I needed to speak to Mr. Christopher. Reluctantly, she got up from her desk and went into his office to tell him that I was waiting to see him. I overheard him say that he didn't have time but to send me in anyway. His opening words to me were, "State your business. Did you write it down?" How condescending to think that I couldn't remember what I wanted to say! Defensively, I replied, "No, I didn't, and what I have to say I don't need to write down!" Pausing a moment to compose myself, I continued, "I came to discuss my demanding schedule." Before I could provide supporting details, he interrupted by saying, "There is nothing more to say about that!" I thought, "If that is his position on the matter, my only recourse is to take my complaint to a higher authority—the Personnel Office!" His closing comment was for me to do whatever I had to do. Then, he dismissed me.

Upon returning to my classroom, I examined the schedule again as though I thought it would magically become more manageable if I stared at it long enough. Perhaps, I needed a few minutes to digest my encounter with Mr. Christopher and plan my strategy with personnel. Whatever the case, I successfully made it through the remainder of the school day, planning activities as though I were going to be there. However, in my heart, I knew the contrary.

Before the end of the school day, word had spread like wild fire that I was dissatisfied with my schedule. One of the white teachers (and seventh-grade department chairperson), who bravely greeted me during our first staff meeting, approached me as I was exiting the building to ask about my displeasure. It did not surprise me that she knew about my situation, but the speed at which my response to it reached her was a bit startling! She concurred with me that my assignment was a heavy load for a first-year teacher and offered to help me make it work. I appreciated her offer, but I had decided that Hooper Alexander Elementary School was not the place for me. Unbeknownst to the teacher, I had one foot out of the door and the other one on a banana peel! Mr. Christopher saw us talking; cut me a piercing look without exchanging words, then walked to his car. I spent a few more minutes talking to my department chair before departing for personnel.

As I drove from the school's parking lot, I made a "bee line" to the Personnel Office—at least I thought I had. Being new to the area, I got lost several times and arrived too late to speak to anyone. My plan was to meet with Ms. Diane Carpenter, a white personnel counselor for elementary employment, who had hired and assigned me to Hooper Alexander Elementary School. Surely, she could reassign me. Unable to make any more headway on this matter, I laid it to rest for the evening and went home.

That night, instead of relaxing and unwinding, I played a game of "What If" regarding my impending conversation with Ms. Carpenter. *"What if"* she sided with the Principal and supported his views? *"What if"* she told me that I could not be reassigned? *"What if"* she refused to see me because I hadn't called ahead to schedule an appointment? *"What if"* she decided that I was not the type of teacher that DeKalb needed and terminated me? Needless to say, I didn't get much sleep thinking that I might lose my first professional job since college! Some of my friends were still looking for jobs, and here I was about to lose one! Consoling myself, I decided that if I had to work under the conditions of secret meetings, inflexible administrators, impossible work schedules and rude co-workers, I was better off looking for another job.

The next morning, my top priority was meeting with Ms. Diane Carpenter. I didn't care about reporting late to school, because I knew that I would be transferred—or fired! I arrived earlier than Ms. Carpenter and anxiously awaited her arrival. As she entered the lobby, my heart skipped several beats as I wondered if she would meet with me. My answer came within seconds as she cheerfully greeted me and invited me into her office. She didn't even take time to get settled and drink a cup of coffee! Cutting straight to the chase, she asked how she could be of assistance to me. I started by thanking her for seeing me and by expressing my gratitude for a job with DeKalb Schools. Following her lead—I jumped to the point quickly, telling her that I was regrettably requesting a transfer from Hooper Alexander Elementary School because of the demanding (if not impossible) schedule that I had been given. Listening attentively, she asked to see the schedule. As she studied it, I continued providing details. Realizing that I was the only one talking, I stopped, giving her time to process the schedule. Several minutes later, she questioned what had happened when I talked to the Principal about this situation. "How much should I share with her?" I wondered. Talking to Mr. Christopher proved to be a dead-end. Was I setting myself up for another let-down? Sensing my reservation, Ms. Carpenter leaned forward across her desk and whispered, "Just tell me like it is. I will help you." For some reason, I believed her and disclosed everything!

Her sensitivity to what I was saying was evident by the tears in her eyes. Angrily, she picked up the phone to call Mr. Christopher and to straighten out what she couldn't believe to be true. Suddenly, I got cold feet and pleaded with her not to make the call! "Don't worry. Let me handle it from here," she said, as if on a top-secret mission!

As Ms. Carpenter searched her index for the school's phone number, I wanted her to abort the mission! What was wrong with assigning me to a new school? In my opinion, that would be the best plan for all involved. Obviously, I had opened Pandora's Box and Diane Carpenter was determined to close it!

I sat with bated breath as Ms. Carpenter phoned Hooper Alexander. I thought, "She seems to be making a mountain out of a molehill. All she has to do is reassign me, and we can both get on with our jobs!" The secretary answered the phone and placed Ms. Carpenter on hold for what seemed like hours! Finally, the wait was over when she said, "Good morning, this is Diane Carpenter, and I'm calling to speak to you about one of your staff members, Lonnie Edwards." For the next few moments, there was silence as Mr. Christopher's response was inaudible to me. I don't know what he said, but Ms. Carpenter's next words were explosive! "You just wait a minute, David! Let me tell you how this is going to be handled! Mr. Edwards is a first-year teacher, and nobody is going to make it difficult for him if I have anything to do with it! And I will! If you don't know how to get his schedule straight, I will send one of our Instructional Coordinators to help you with scheduling. This is too much for one person to try to do, and I am going to send him back for you to make his schedule manageable!" With that, she closed with a stern, yet polite, "Thank you, and goodbye."

My heart sank as I heard her say that she was sending me back. I thanked her for intervening on my behalf and requested a transfer in the same breath. Again, she denied my request, but this time she came from behind her desk to sit next to me. I knew we were headed for one of those "this-is-for-your-own-good" sermons! She said, "Mr. Edwards, I have a daughter in teaching, and I am very much aware of the fact that things don't always go as they should. But, when you work at it, things get better. I know this situation seems like a mountain to you right now, and you don't see your way around it. I understand because I've been there myself! Nevertheless, reassignment is not the answer." She continued by telling me how much Hooper Alexander School needed a teacher like me and by affirming her commitment to helping me succeed. Realizing that I had lost the battle of reassignment, I thanked Ms. Carpenter for her help and headed back to the battleground of Hooper Alexander Elementary School.

As I exited Ms. Carpenter's office, I met a lady by the name of Miss Alice Ann Hamilton who was Assistant Director of Personnel. Cordially, she asked my name and how I was enjoying my assignment. I introduced myself and told her that I felt marginally optimistic about my challenges at my school, but that Ms. Carpenter had been a tremendous help to me. Miss Hamilton assured me that I was in good hands with Ms. Carpenter. Curious to know what my problems were at Hooper Alexander School, she took a little longer with me to explore the situation. Miss Hamilton told me that she had heard of me through Mr. Wilburn Adams, the Associate Superintendent who had recruited me. I briefed Miss Hamilton on my concerns and thanked her for listening. As I slowly walked out of the Personnel Office, I overheard Ms. Carpenter telling Miss Hamilton, "We are going to make sure that Mr. Edwards is successful." With that, I drove back to school feeling some comfort in finding two allies.

5

Back on the Battlefield

On the way back to Hooper Alexander, reality hit and my conscience began to counsel me. What was normally a 10-minute drive took over 40 minutes because I stopped several times to write a resignation letter. My "Plan B" was to look for another job, if things didn't improve at Hooper—even with the help of my allies in Personnel! As I sat in the car, I drafted several letters, but none was satisfactory. I discarded them as quickly as I wrote them.

Frustrated with my attempts to explain why I was leaving, I stopped for a moment to pray. In my heart, I knew that quitting was not the answer; never before in my life had I given up. I was not a quitter! However, this challenge seemed bigger than me, and short of quitting, I didn't know what else to do. I prayed a familiar prayer, asking God for wisdom and courage to challenge this situation with tact and diplomacy. As I prayed, I drove slowly toward Hooper. When I arrived in the parking lot, I sat for a few moments wondering what to expect when I reported to the Principal. Taking a deep breath and stepping out of the car, I decided not to let him upset me or threaten me because of my trip to the Personnel Office. After all, if my trip had been as successful as I thought it had been, Ms. Carpenter and Miss Hamilton would handle one step out of line from him.

When I entered the building, I went to my classroom. I had more time to collect my thoughts, as well as to get on with the business of planning my classes, if I were to stay there. Within ten minutes, the secretary via the public address system summoned me to the Principal's office. I left my room immediately, but sauntered to the office. As I approached the front office, I was greeted by the senior black teacher, Ms. Thomas, who whispered to me that she wanted me to be professional and polite in doing whatever it was that I had to do. Smiling, I thanked her and continued moving toward the Principal's office.

Mr. Christopher met me in the main office and asked, "What are we going to do with this problem?" "I don't have a problem. You have both the problem and the solution!" I retorted. He did not respond to my comments and walked us into his office. It was obvious to me that he was upset that I had gone beyond his building-level authority seeking a resolution that he had no intention of giving.

Abruptly switching gears from our heated interaction, he pulled out his master schedule and compared it with mine. He then called the secretary and requested that she contact the sixth-grade teachers. Shortly thereafter, one of the teachers showed up for the conference. After a brief discussion, my schedule was adjusted to a more reasonable assignment. This teacher, Ms. Smith, never asked one question as to why the change was necessary which led me to believe that a prior conference had been held. At the close of the meeting, Mr. Christopher asked if I was pleased with my schedule. I answered "No," but added that I was willing to try it since he had given the math assignment back to the sixth-grade teachers. Ms. Smith then looked over at me for the first time and said she would be glad to help me in any other way she could. She added that she had asked Mr. Christopher for the change because she didn't think the children wanted to have her as a teacher two years in a row; she had had them as fifth graders. Mr. Christopher thanked Ms. Smith for coming and asked her to coordinate her schedule with the other sixth-grade teachers so that one of them would go out to P.E. each day to assist me with the supervision of the children. She reluctantly said she would. In addition, Mr. Christopher requested that she bring him the name of each teacher expected to go out to P.E. with me each day.

After Ms. Smith had left the meeting, he called the secretary into his office to give her the changes and requested that she retype them and put a copy in the mailbox of each sixth- and seventh-grade teacher. He also requested that she contact the other two seventh-grade teachers and have them report to his office. Two to three minutes later, they entered his office, sat directly in front of me, and yet, did not speak to me. It was obvious to me that they knew some changes were about to occur and that they were not in favor of them!

Mr. Christopher began explaining that the reason they were there was to re-work their schedules. One of the teachers never looked up, but commented sarcastically, "Go ahead and do what you have to do." The Principal continued, "I am giving each of you one of the reading classes that I had scheduled for Mr. Edwards, and the two of you will rotate going out to P.E. with him to assist with supervision." He told them that he wanted to see the rotation schedule by 4:00 o'clock that afternoon. There were no questions nor any discussion about the changes. As the two teachers were leaving the office, one of them — Ms. Cooley, who was serving as 7th grade chairperson, told me that there would be a departmental meeting the next morning at 10:00 a.m. and asked if I would attend. I answered that I would and asked where it would convene. As she left the office, she replied that it would be in her room, number 10, on the front hall. Mr. Christopher stood by the door and told them everything would be just fine; that they would see how this worked out, and if it didn't, he would make the necessary adjustments.

After they left, he closed the door, and said to me, "Mr. Edwards, I'm sorry this problem occurred and even more so that you felt the need to go down to the Central Office (Personnel)." I had nothing to say in response to his comment. He told me if other problems occurred, he wanted the privilege of trying to correct it without involving anyone else. "Privilege" he called it. It was clear that he was telling me not to go over his head again! As long as we could work things out, he didn't have to worry about that. So, I agreed to honor his request.

Mr. Christopher wanted to review my schedule a second time to verify the changes. At this point, he seemed overly anxious to appease me. He assured me that he had done the best he could and stated that he had made a few people upset because of the changes. As much as I tried not to respond to what I considered confrontational statement, I felt his comment merited at least a brief reply. So, I said, "Mr. Christopher, I hope we are privileged to work together long enough to learn to respect, trust and support each other, and the fact that some individuals are upset over your efforts to be fair to me should not be a worry to you. It should be a confirmation of how justice and injustice can co-exist. I hope that this experience is the beginning of your understanding of what it feels like to take a stand against someone who would choose to be unfair to another." Judging by the baffled look on his face, I could tell that he didn't have a clue about what I was trying to tell him. I assured him that I would help him to overcome this challenge by working with him and the Hooper Alexander staff and winning them over. (I considered his lack of sensitivity to the injustices shown to me to be a social challenge.)

Having had his fill of my soapbox preaching, Mr. Christopher stood up and walked over to the door indicating that this meeting was over. I politely dismissed myself, and he wished me the best as I left. For a moment, I felt like the battle was over; at least the one with Mr. Christopher was. Whether he was sincere in his effort to help was secondary to the fact that he was behaving like someone who cared. Having cleared that major hurdle, I was confident that I could face whatever came next!

6

Preplanning:
Preparing for the Students

With the battle of leaving or staying now over, I had to get on with the business of preparing to teach. As a new teacher, I welcomed any help I could get; but, there was little help available — or at least that I felt comfortable seeking. Coming to this realization reminded me that struggles were not yet over. I thought to myself, "How am I to develop an acceptable—better yet— outstanding set of lesson plans for Mr. Christopher overnight?" In my dark moment of distress, a lightbulb popped on! I had lesson plans! They were at home somewhere; they had been given to me weeks earlier.

The day I was hired, I met Ms. Narvie Harris, the first black Instructional Coordinator for DeKalb County Schools, as I was leaving the Central Office. After a brief conversation, Ms. Harris invited me into her office to discuss my lesson plans. I had none since I had just been hired. When she found this out, she took me under her wings and spent the next hour writing out three weeks of plans for me. Initially, I was perturbed by her assumption that I couldn't develop my own plans, but having other things on my mind, such as living arrangements, I didn't offer any resistance. After she had completed the plans, I grudgingly accepted them, thanked her for her interest and put them away somewhere. I could not have imagined how valuable the time I spent with her would be and how it would contribute to my preplanning success.

Needless to say, I rushed back home that evening, desperately looking for those golden lesson plans. Upon finding them, I felt as happy as if I had found a one hundred-dollar bill—back in those days. I spent half the night working from those plans, getting ready for the next day because Mr. Christopher was going to review them to determine my readiness for the students the following week.

I reported for work early that Friday morning so that I could arrange the students' chairs as well as my desk. I put the name of each student on the blackboard, according to the rows of chairs. As soon as that task was completed, Mr. Christopher called me to the office and requested that I bring my checklist with me.

As I entered his office, he greeted me with a very warm "Good morning" and asked me to have a seat. There was no small talk as he got right to business. His first question was, "Have you got your lesson plans prepared for Monday morning and for the entire week?" Proudly, I replied, "Yes sir," and passed them to him. He began asking questions about each Goal and Objective. His questions seemed more like a pop-quiz to catch me unprepared than a sincere effort to ensure my readiness for class. To his second question, "Do you have a chair for each student on your class register?", my reply was, "Yes sir, I have a chair for each student recorded on my homeroom rollbook." His third question was, "Do you have all of your sixth-grade health and seventh-grade science books?" My answer was, "Yes sir." His fourth and last question was, "Are you ready for your Physical Education classes?" Again, I answered affirmatively pointing out that the Physical Education classes were going to be large, with three classes coming each period, without their teachers (which would be about seventy to eighty students per grade level). He leaned back in his chair; took off his glasses and said, "Mr. Edwards, this schedule looks fine to me. You know, I have done all I care to do at this time to help you fit in on this staff. So, you might just have to get started, and if you need help, let me know and I will look at it later."

At that point, I was sure he was having trouble with the staff; I was not going to add more fuel to the fire. I said it was not a real issue; I just wanted him to know that I might need some assistance with that many children at one time since there was no gymnasium. I let him know that I understood his position. I said that I would get started and would keep him informed. As I walked toward the door to leave his office, he asked me to remember our earlier agreement about letting him work at resolving matters on the staff before I made any other decision. He walked over to the door and extended his hand. We shook hands, and I headed back to my classroom. I thought what a pseudo gesture it had been, but at least he had shaken my hand.

When I stopped by the teachers' lounge to get a Coke, there was much discussion going on among the sixth-and seventh-grade teachers. However, once they saw me, their conversation ended. I got my Coke; no one spoke, and I left the lounge. I imagined I must have been the main topic of discussion. This was a strange environment for a new teacher. I thought, "My God, they (my student-teacher supervisors) didn't tell me how to deal with this type of administrative and peer behavior." Having been a successful high school and college athlete, I knew that I understood teamwork, but this new profession called "teaching" seemed to have few team players, if any. Or, at least for the time being, I had not met any on the Hooper Alexander staff.

Just before lunch, Ms. White, a veteran white teacher who was more liberal than others, stopped by my room to see how I was doing. I was so shocked, but glad, to see a friendly face that I almost fell out of my chair trying to get up to greet her. I wanted to hug her, but I knew that gesture of affection was far from appropriate. We shook hands, and I insisted that she sit down. She smiled and said she had only a few minutes but wanted to know if she could help me in any way. I immediately said, "Yes, please look over what I have done." She laughed and said, "Let's just work on this bulletin board for a while." We proceeded to re-arrange the message and items on the board. She complimented my work and said it looked good, but it needed just a little sprucing up. She shared other ideas and suggested that I consider her as a mentor. She said she would re-check all of my plans of operation before they were executed, and just maybe that would assist me in having a successful career beginning. I was so surprised by her statement that it took me a moment to respond. Suspicion resurfaced, as I wondered if she was an assigned "spy" chosen to check up on me, then report my shortcomings to the Principal .... all of my shortcomings. I thought, "Well, if she helps me to correct them, what will it matter?" I graciously accepted her support and showed her my schedule. She agreed with everything but the size of my P.E. classes, asking if I had anyone going out to P.E. with me. I said, "No." She asked if the Principal was aware of that problem. I told her that he was and had promised to make some adjustments with that part of my schedule. Ms. White added that this was important because managing a large number of children could be challenging as well as frightening. One mistake could possibly cost me my job! With racial tension as heated as it was at the time, many parents were looking for one mistake to blow out of proportion. At that point, I realized that she was genuine in her mission to help me get off to a good start.

For the next twenty minutes, Ms. White inquired about each activity I had planned for Physical Education. She asked what activities I had planned for the boys; then, for the girls, and what activity would they perform together? I shared

a few: I had a daily ten-minute struct   )ination of aerobic
movements; and rhythm and dance ex   eyes widened, and
she immediately focused on rhythm, a   orld are you going to
do with these children that involves   efore I could respond,
she said, "You had better re-think this   of your activities. An
activity that might call for students to touch each oth   could be a very sensitive
matter for some students and their parents." Condescendingly, she asked, "What
kind of dance would you teach, anyway?" I thought, "How dare she assume that
I was incapable of instructing dance!"   Confidently, I answered, "Square
dancing." Her mouth fell open, and she said, "What did you say? Square
dancing?" I repeated, "Yes, square dancing." She cautioned me that this activity
could cost me my job. Suddenly, I wasn't feeling the same support from my
"mentor" as I had in the beginning of this conversation. Ms. White stated she
would not even consider such an activity at the elementary level and asked me to
justify my reasons for such an activity.

I took the liberty of being a little more comprehensive with my answer. I
said, "First, I am aware this will be a new activity for these students, but it's great
for young children to learn through participation. Square dancing has four
components I would like to teach them: (1) how to listen and react—cognitive
development; (2) how to follow a consistent and patterned movement—physical
development; (3) how to cooperate with each other—behavioral development,
and (4) how to get along with others—social development." I concluded my
argument by emphasizing that we all could stand some improvement in these
various areas of development. Defending my activity a step further, I pointed out
that the children would develop many other skills such as physical balance, self-
confidence, and leadership.

Ms. White sat quietly for a moment, leaning back in her chair as if to be
soaking in what she had just heard. Abruptly switching gears from my schedule
and its rationale, she asked, "Where did you go to college?" "University of
Montevallo in Montevallo, Alabama," I answered. She asked me to tell her a
little about it. Not knowing the reason for her question, jokingly, I asked if she
had two years to listen. I could tell her stories about my college experience that
would make her cringe! Obviously not in the mood for my levity, she said she
didn't have that much time, but wanted to know more about my background. I
asked her if it was because I was going to teach square dance. She smiled,
saying, "No," but instantly changed it to "Yes."

I was beginning to feel quite comfortable with Ms. White, so I decided to tell her a little about Montevallo. I started at the beginning, telling her that I was the first black male student to sign an athletic scholarship with the university in the Spring of 1969. She interrupted, "Is that where you learned how to square dance?" I told her it was. Although I was ready to tell her much more, that seemed to be all she needed to know to feel comfortable about my credentials. With a sigh of relief she said, "I know there is something unique about you, and I wish you a lot of luck. Go ahead with your plans. They look very good but be careful with this square dancing, and if I can help, let me know. But, before I go, let me warn you about turning in your reports and your rollbook. Let me check it to make sure that everything is done correctly until I am sure that you have the hang of things." I thanked her for lending a helping hand and assured her that I would let her double-check everything. After she left, I continued to get things ready for the students. Excitement was mounting as I felt that I was on track and that things might be fine at Hooper after a rocky start.

Around three o'clock that afternoon, Mr. Christopher stopped by my room to conduct a final assessment of my readiness for the students on Monday morning. His assessment lasted for about five minutes, and I received a "Satisfactory" rating on everything. He said he had worked it out where one teacher on each grade level would rotate and accompany me with the large P.E. classes. He thought this would help in the area of management and supervision. I thanked him, and he pleasantly shook my hand. He said he was pleased with my planning and organization and wished me a good weekend along with good luck with my new profession. His behavior was at least a 180-degree turn from our initial meetings. There was still much room for improvement, but I knew a victory when I saw one! For the moment, I had aborted my plans for a transfer. Hope prevailed that I could be successful at Hooper Alexander and make a difference in the lives of its students.

This particular day was full of surprises. Before I left that evening, a black man named Mr. Eugene Thompson walked into my room and introduced himself as the Physical Education Coordinator for the school system. The purpose of his visit was to assist me in any way possible to have a successful P.E. program for the students at Hooper Alexander. Mr. Thompson pointed out the areas in which I would be evaluated later in the year. The five main areas were safety, planning, organization, execution, and supervision. While he made me feel comfortable, his expressions sent a strong message that he was very serious about his job. It was clear that Mr. Thompson wanted me to succeed, but I was going to have to work hard to do it! He asked to see my lesson plans and to show him where I would conduct my classes — during pleasant weather and during inclement weather.

After a brief review of my plans and a general survey of the P.E. field and equipment, he looked directly in my face, put his hands on my shoulders and said, "Mr. Edwards, you have done a very good job preparing for the students. Your preparation looks as good, if not better, than any I have observed this week, and that includes thirty or more elementary schools." He added that for a first-year teacher, my preparation was outstanding and that if I implemented and executed it half as well as it looked on paper, the children at Hooper were in for a real treat!

Before I could thank him for his positive assessment, he interrupted me, put his arm around my shoulder and said, "Mr. Edwards, you are one of a handful of black P.E. teachers in this whole county and the first black male, ever, for this school and community. You will have a big job breaking down social barriers that we have been dealing with for years. You will have to stand up for what is best and do the right thing for all children. Some people will have trouble with you only because you are black — not the children as much as some of their parents. But, if you stay focused on the children and win them over, you will get the parents."

He walked away about four or five steps, turned around and walked back to me — this time with tears forming in his eyes. He again placed both of his hands on my shoulders and solemnly spoke, "Lonnie, you have got to make this work; you have got to love all these children no matter what conditions you encounter. I am counting on you to deal with it to the best of your abilities, and I will do all I can to help." He paused and said, "You must handle this very professionally, and put your best foot forward every day. Turn all of your reports in on time; have them done in ink—make sure it is blue or black ink."

And finally, he said, "Let me ask about this unit on square dancing I see here in your plans. Do you know how to square dance?" I looked at Mr. Thompson, smiled, and said, "Yes, sir." He smiled, "cut a few steps" and said this could be something if I stayed with it and made sure that everyone participated. He asked me why I thought square dancing would be valuable to my P.E. program. For the next five minutes, I gave him the same explanation I had given Ms. White that morning. When I finished giving my rationale, Mr. Thompson jumped straight up, stuck out his hand and said, "Give me five." We slapped hands, and he said I was a 'bad dude' and 'had my stuff together' — implying that I was well-prepared. Then, he became serious again and said, "Mr. Edwards, don't *make* the children square dance; teach them why it's good for them and encourage them to participate. You can catch more flies with honey than you can with vinegar." I thought about that analogy for a moment, and though I did not understand what he meant at the time, I knew it would become crystal clear to me later. Before leaving, Mr. Thompson asked if I had any questions. I said that I didn't. My comment was that I would like for him to keep in touch with me from time to time to see how I was doing. He agreed. As he walked out the door, he looked back and said, "Lonnie, be careful, and good luck."

By this time, it was nearly five o'clock — an hour after 'quitting time' — and more than half of the teachers were still there. As I went to close my homeroom door, I met Mr. Christopher coming out of the office. He said, "I thought you were gone already." I said, "No, sir. Mr. Eugene Thompson from the county office was here and wanted to see the P.E. area, plans and equipment." Mr. Christopher said he was sure that Mr. Thompson had been impressed. He left me by bidding me a good weekend. I wasn't sure what the weekend had in store, but it was certainly off to a terrific start!

7

Making Friends

On my way to the parking lot to go home for the weekend, I noticed four fifth- or sixth-grade white boys playing ball on the school's basketball court. Upon seeing me, they stopped playing and ran over to tell me that they had heard about my being their new P. E. coach. "We're glad you are coming, and we sure hope you are better than that other P.E. coach we had last year 'cause he didn't know how to do nothing!", one student commented. Another chimed in, "We could beat him playing everything! Can you play?" A third student challenged, " Come on. Let us try you first." While I really didn't feel like it at the moment, I knew it was a great opportunity to start making friends and who better to have as friends than the children? They didn't know, at the time, that I had just completed a collegiate basketball career and just three months earlier had been cut from the Chicago Bulls rookie camp. I was much too advanced for them, but they didn't know, and I didn't tell them. This was not so much a game of basketball as it was going to be a game of relationship building.

Setting my books in the car while opening the trunk to get my gym shoes, I began teasing them about the beating that was in store for them—a common sporting strategy known as "getting your bluff in." They laughed and chose sides, selecting a three-on-two team and giving me the boy who couldn't play that well. This little boy didn't want to play with me, but he didn't have much choice because the others did not choose him. So, we got together to work out our game strategy. The plan was simple. We only needed to decide who was going to take the ball out and when to pass the ball back to me.

The game began. From the start, I was being double-teamed, but they were not having any success stopping me from shooting and making baskets. After losing the first two games, all three of the boys on the opposite team decided that they were just going to try to check or block me—in other words, when the double-team strategy didn't work, they shifted to a triple-team approach, bringing in the alternate as a permanent player. Sadly for them, the competition was still too great! Even my inept teammate gave a surprising performance. I made several under-the-basket passes to him, and he caught a few, shooting them successfully into the basket! He shocked himself so much with his own performance that I thought the whole neighborhood heard him as he yelled, "We are tearing you guys up!"

After the third game, I stopped and told them that I had to go. It was about six o'clock, but they wanted just one more game as a last ditch effort to win at least one game. When I agreed to one more game, the strategic planning I saw going on among those three boys was amazing! They wanted to win so badly that they had decided that one of them was going to hold my hands to stop me from shooting! They did so every chance they got! In my heart, I wanted them to win and was tempted to blow the game, but I thought about what they had said about the previous P.E. teacher not knowing "nothing", so I had to beat them a fourth time. My teammate was ecstatic with the results, but our competitors were frustrated, disappointed and amazed that they had lost all four games! Obviously, they had no clue that an "old man" like me would be a match for their youth!

All of the boys shook hands with me as they left the court. I overheard one of them saying that I must be a pro but didn't tell them because I seldom missed a shot. "Man, he is real rough!" was another comment made. I left the court laughing to myself and feeling very concerned for my little partner because he was kidding the other boys to such a degree that I thought that if he didn't temper his kidding, he might have a little trouble before he got home. I got in my car and pulled off, heading for home—a little tired, but it had been worth it. I needed the exercise, and I could count on having four new friends Monday morning.

That weekend, I spent a lot of time reflecting on the things that had transpired thus far and anticipating the students' arrival. As I reflected on the events of the day — three conferences with Mr. Christopher; the quizzing, assessing and inspection of plans by Ms. White; then, doing the same thing again with Mr. Thompson — it was no wonder that I felt mentally drained. It had really been a tough day! I thought about one of my grandmother's sayings that she used when things were real tough, "You'd much rather go before the president for having 'stole' a government mule than get a whipping from me!" Well, I don't think I thoroughly understand that analogy yet, but I know that on that particular day, I felt as though I had faced the nation to defend my position on why I chose teaching as a second career. The bright spot was that I had successfully passed all scrutiny with flying colors.

When I thought about what the boys on the basketball court had told me about their last P.E. teacher, I was confident that I had made a different, indelible impression on them! Knowing how fast the kid "grapevine" travels, I was curious to know what type of reputation I would have with the students on Monday, especially since my team had won all four games. That was a pleasant and informative activity because it answered some of my questions concerning the probing investigation I had encountered that day.

I summed up the day as having been a total success, and just before I drifted off to sleep, I thanked God for His help and that of Ms. Narvie Harris who had taken the time to give me my lesson plan structure the first day I was employed. I cringed when I thought about what I had started to do with those plans after she gave them to me. That I will not tell, but what I will say is that had it not been for Ms. Harris, it would have been more career threatening to confront the assessment I had gone through that day. What a challenge!

And, the best was yet to come .... the students on Monday morning!

8

The First Day of School

At last! That long-awaited day for me to start my professional career as a classroom teacher had arrived. All that I had heard, read and imagined was now staring me in the face. Like most first-year teachers, I thought that I had the blueprint on how to teach. I thought that I could literally change the whole world, and that my big chance to do it was here. However, no one had ever mentioned the dynamics of intra-staff relations among teachers; nor that one's race would be such an issue in the teaching profession. No one mentioned that one could be called one of "them" and for the most part, be put on display like a trophy in a case, to be observed everyday as though they were the *missing link* of the human race.

After my initial interactions during preplanning, I thought that my presence was reasonably accepted since everyone had been made aware that I was officially employed and going to be on the Hooper Alexander staff. Little did I know that this was just the beginning. I had not met many of the parents — maybe just a few during preplanning — and I had no clue about the concept of "parent-teacher politics." This is where a teacher or a small group of teachers, mainly veteran teachers connected through the PTA, have established such a close relationship that all the staff news and interactions are shared for both positive and negative reasons.   The grapevine and the "street committee" chairperson had obviously done a great job circulating the word that they were going to have a black boy/man as the P.E. teacher. It appeared that everybody in the community — parents-grandparents-neighbors, and even distant relatives — were present to witness, first-hand, my appearance on the first day of school.

I arrived on the Hooper campus for work that Monday morning around 7:30 a.m. (which was thirty minutes earlier than reporting time), and it took me almost ten minutes to find a parking space. There was a slight traffic jam in the parking lot because many parents were dropping off their children while others were trying to park.   There were no crossing guards or police directing traffic; therefore, traffic and parking was a free-for-all! Throughout this entire ordeal, I had observed two black families who seemed to know where they were going because they had upper-elementary-age children. They seemed happy to see me and said, "Good morning. We are sure glad to see you. Your name is all over the community, and we heard about you while shopping this weekend." They extended their hands to shake mine and introduced themselves. The first lady was Ms. Earnestine Hunter who had three children with her; the second lady was Ms. Charlotte Stokes who had one child in tow. We shook hands, and they wished me the best of luck.

While walking into the building, I overheard someone say, "Here he comes!", and it seemed like all eyes, up and down the hall, were on me. I acted as though I hadn't heard a thing and continued down the hall as if walking down a receiving line. It felt more like walking down the middle of two receiving lines because people were lined up on both sides of the hall. I was smiling graciously, and occasionally, would nod and say, "Good morning" to someone while looking that person straight in the eyes. Not one black family was standing along the walls. The ones I had met outside went a different direction when we got in the building. However, this experience didn't phase me at all. Those who were there with intimidation in mind were about two-and-a-half years too late. The Montevallo experience had matured me in the ways of racial, cultural and social awareness. Thank God for the Montevallo experience! Otherwise, I might have turned around and headed back to Mississippi!

Everyone signed in for work at the main office. A line had already formed by the time I arrived. One of the two teachers standing in front of me, waiting to sign in, was on my grade level. No one spoke. My grade-level colleague looked at me; turned her head toward the wall; signed in and walked out. There were a few parents in the office looking for directions on registering their children, and they stopped to focus on me. By this time, I was next to sign in. I picked up the pen, signed in at 7:45 a.m. and walked over to the teachers' mailboxes to get my class rollbook. The Principal was standing there. He nodded and said, "Good morning." "Good morning. Thank you." I replied. He bid me a good day, and as I turned to exit the office, I faced a crowd who seemed to be watching my every move. I headed for the door, and they parted a path as though I were a police officer. I went to the left out of the office and headed to my homeroom, which was three doors down on the right. The hall was now crowded with parents and students standing around every door, looking for their names on the lists posted there; particularly, the students who had been there the previous year.

I entered my room at 7:50 a.m. A few students were ready and sitting at their desks. Others were moving from row to row after seeing where their names were listed on the blackboard. I set my books on my desk, and when I turned around to go to the door, another crowd was standing there looking me over. I walked to the door, this time with my hand extended toward the parents to greet them. Many would not shake hands, but, instead, nodded at me. Finally, Ms. Padget, a parent with five children, shook my hand and said in front of the crowd, "I am glad that you are here. Welcome." That seemed to break the ice for many of them, and from that moment on, even some of the children who entered the room would shake my hand. Finally, the bell rang. It was eight o'clock and students had five minutes to scurry to their homeroom classes. When the bell rang, I was standing at the door, observing the crowd and listening to some parents who were still exclaiming, "That's him!" Occasionally, one would stop and shake my hand.

It appeared that five percent of the parents were black and new to the school. Many had not preregistered their children and needed to know where to go and what to do. By the time four or five black families had stopped to ask me for directions, I overheard a passerby say, "Look! They are already gathering." I knew this was a bad idea. My "saving grace" was the announcement Mr. Christopher made via the public address system, directing all new parents and students who had not registered to go to the cafeteria which was located in front of the Principal's office.

While directing some of the black parents toward the cafeteria, one after the other would ask me to look after their children at school. Apparently, they perceived me to be the guardian over their children since I was the only black male teacher on staff. They saw me as their ally and felt that as long as I was there and watching over their children, justice would be served.

My guardianship was put to the test, immediately, as I had to intercede between irate black parents and the Principal. Almost simultaneously, two parents walked up to me; talking loudly and obviously highly upset over the fact that they had stood in the front office for nearly ten minutes and hadn't registered their children yet. They insisted that all whites at the school were pure racists and that I had better watch my back before they tried to harm me. (Little did they know that I had already fought my first battle with this staff and felt quite victorious.) I tried calming them down, but by this time, Mr. Christopher had heard the loud noise in the hall and came out of his office to see what the commotion was about. The parent who was the most irritated yelled, "You racist pig! Get out of my face before I destroy you!" Mr. Christopher moved a few steps away from this parent while explaining what had happened. His effort was to no avail because this parent was not listening to him. A number of teachers and students ran to the door to see what was going on. It was obvious that Mr. Christopher was frightened by this parent's antagonistic behavior. I wasn't sure what to do, so I said, "Sir, let me try to help you." The parent (a black male) turned toward me and asked, "What are you going to do? You are a black man like me, and this man is a redneck." We looked each other directly in the face, and he said, "I am from Detroit, and I am not used to mess like this." I said, "There is a better way to deal with a matter like this. Let me see how I can help." The man calmed down, and Mr. Christopher directed me to help the parent. "I will get someone to cover your class," he said with a sigh of relief. Getting someone to cover my class was a far easier task than dealing with this irate parent!

Politely, I requested that this gentleman and the other parents follow me to the cafeteria as I directed teachers and students to return to their classrooms. To my surprise, everybody responded. This parent looked at Mr. Christopher and said, "I'm glad that at least you are smart enough to have somebody on this staff who knows how to talk to people, but I'm not finished with you. I'm going to the Board of Education to report this mess and that we have a redneck for a Principal!" Mr. Christopher appeared intimidated by the parent's threats. I felt like a referee in a boxing match, separating the contenders and sending them to neutral corners! I sent Mr. Christopher back to his office, assuring him that I had everything under control. I took the parent with me to the cafeteria, promising him that we would work things out, if he would just give us the chance.

When the parents and I arrived at the cafeteria, I directed them to have a seat (everyone complied peacefully). For the moment, I was a hero for managing what could have been a mob situation! I was pretty proud of my performance, but didn't know what to do next. Now that the parents were calmly assembled in the cafeteria, what was I do to with them? Though I had demonstrated that I was fairly adept in race relations, I didn't know the first thing about registering children for school! My job was done as far as I was concerned. Now that the parents were settled in the cafeteria, the staff who handled registration could do their job. I needed to get on with the business of teaching. In all my detailed lesson plans, there was no mention of handling school registration!

I left the parents in the cafeteria and returned to the main office to tell them that the ball was in their court. All they needed to do was to send someone to the cafeteria to assist the parents who were waiting patiently to enroll their children in school. As I entered the office, Mr. Christopher was standing there shuffling some papers in his hands. Before I could tell him that I had completed my mission and that I was on my way back to my classroom, he said, "I have your class covered for right now. I want you to help me to resolve this matter." I was startled because I thought my work was done and because he knew that I didn't know what to do!

Sensing my discomfort with registering students, Mr. Christopher coached me through the process. He gave me some forms from the stack of papers in his hand to take to parents to complete and requested that I return them immediately to him. I must have made ten trips from his office to the cafeteria, and after about thirty minutes, it was over. The perturbed parent and I were now talking calmly, and I was showing him how to get his fourth- and fifth-graders to their classes. By this time, we were talking as though we were friends. I encouraged him to apologize to the Principal because the registration process at every school is frustrating. Additionally, I asked if he would mind doing so in the presence of his children. I thought that this would be good role modeling. Since his children were present when he threatened the Principal and called him names, they needed to learn how to fix such altercations. He didn't like the idea, but agreed. I was ecstatic; besides, stopping by the main office to see the Principal bought me a little more time to find my way to the fourth- and fifth-grade hall.

I found Mr. Christopher who was busily running errands in the halls and trying to get students to their classrooms. I stopped him and asked if I could interrupt him for just a moment. Appreciative of all the assistance I had given him that day, he graciously paused to attend to my request. First, I asked where the fourth- and fifth-grade hall was, and he smiled and teased, "You don't know? You seem to be doing well with everything else." Then, he pointed to the right for fifth grade and to the left for fourth grade. I smiled, somewhat embarrassed, because the fifth grade was just four doors down from mine. Secondly, I informed him that the parent I had been working with wanted to have a word with him. I asked if he would step into the cafeteria where this parent was waiting. I told him that this gentleman wanted to apologize to him for his indignant behavior. Mr. Christopher appeared stunned asking, "What parent?" How could he have forgotten that quickly the incident that pulled me away from my class? Had he realized that I had not met one of my students yet, because he had other teachers covering my class?

Before I could recount the incident, the parent had found his way to us in the hall. He approached us and humbly addressed Mr. Christopher, saying, "I want to express my apology for giving you a hard time this morning. I guess the tension got the best of me." He extended his hand to the Principal and they shook as if reaching a peace treaty. I think in a way they had. Mr. Christopher smiled and agreed with the parent that registration had been frustrating. He said that this was the largest crowd he had ever seen! The parent thanked me for helping him and his children get settled in school and for introducing them to Mr. Christopher. Finally, I gave him directions to his children's classrooms. That seemed to end that chapter of my morning.

In my opinion, this ordeal had ended in great victories for all of us: for the parent—maturity, recovery of self-control and positive role modeling for his children; for Mr. Christopher— psychological recovery from embarrassment and fear of future involvement with this parent; for the children, a great example of adults — one black and the other white — being able to resolve confrontational matters quiescently; and for me, satisfaction of having been successful, not only in showing leadership at a very sensitive moment, but also in bridging a relationship between black and white adults.

The bell rang, signaling the end of first-period class, and I had not yet met my students. Had only one period passed? The events of the morning seemed like hours! As the parent was on his way out of the building, he waved and yelled, "Good luck to you guys." Mr. Christopher and I were now standing together and feeling pleased that a bad situation had been remedied and was behind us. He looked at me with comfort, and said, "Mr. Edwards, thanks a million. You have done a week's work. Too bad this is not the weekend. Well, you go and take your class, and if you are half as good with children as you have been this morning with upset parents, we are in for a great school year." I thanked him for his vote of confidence. The bell rang, and I went to take my second-period class.

When I entered my classroom, the Librarian who had been there for my homeroom and first-period classes seemed happy to see me. (I'm sure she was relieved that I finally showed up to do my job! Just as registering students was not in my lesson plans, teaching my classes was not in hers!) She took the liberty of introducing me to my students and sharing with them that I had been helping the Principal. I just stood there and listened to her kind remarks while wondering what had caused her change of behavior. She graciously showed me the roll book and told me that she hadn't started anything I would have to undo. I walked her to the door and thanked her for managing my class. It was show time for me! Regardless of the other distractions of the morning, meeting my students and getting on with the business of teaching was the main attraction!

I closed the door, walked back to my desk, and started my class by having each student stand and give a brief self-introduction. I had thirty-two students; two of whom were black and, seemingly, quite reserved. The white students seemed uncertain about what to expect from me. Some even appeared frightened when I called their names during the self-introductions. When they had all introduced themselves, it was my turn. I introduced myself and gave a general overview of my expectations that included everything from not talking in class to getting permission to go to the restroom. Since this period was a science class, I felt compelled to at least distribute the textbook we would be using. Because I hadn't done any teaching yet, this was my way of feeling like I was jumping right into the pool.

Once the books were issued, I allotted the remainder of the class period for questions. No one made a sound. I tried to ignite the conversation by asking who had heard that I had beaten three of their classmates playing basketball. Every hand flew into the air, including the two black students. For the first time that period, I saw smiles coming from over half of the class. "Well," I thought, "I have pushed the right button. They are responding." I randomly selected five or six of them, including both black students, to share with the rest of the class what they had heard. Each student reported as though he had been there watching the game. They made statements like, "You are very strong and rough" ... "You have some big muscles" ... "You like children"... "You love basketball and should be a pro," and the final statement was actually a question (which had nothing to do with basketball) ... "Why did you come here?"

The tone of the conversation shifted from jovial to serious. I explained that I had just finished college and had selected teaching as a second career choice. Before I could finish, the bell rang, but nobody moved. It was so quiet in the room that you could have heard a pin fall on the floor. The clamor in the hall by other students trying to get to their next class was quite audible! However, I told the students that we would have to continue this discussion later.

I directed my class to get their belongings from under their desks, to stand up and quietly form a single-file line. By this time, Mr. Christopher was walking down the hall trying to direct students to where they needed to be. He looked in my room and observed the calm students. They were so still that, at first, he didn't think anyone was in there. In the students' presence, he complimented me, "Great job. This is how it ought to be." At that moment, I didn't know who was prouder — the class or me! I thanked him, walked over to the door where he was and gave dismissal direction. As the students filed out, a number of them looked at me and said that they really liked the class and that they were glad I was there. One of the black students, a young man, shook my hand and said, "Give me five" — meaning to hit him in his hand — and that started a chain reaction with the next eight to ten young men. Mr. Christopher observed this happening and said, "I am overwhelmed with what control you seem to have with people." What he labeled as "control" was simply respect. Adults and children respond favorably when they have been shown that they are important and valued.

One of the seventh-grade teachers who hadn't spoken to me the previous week was approaching the door for the next class and, overhearing Mr. Christopher's statement, said "Good morning. You are going to be a real help around here." I was confused as to the meaning of her statement, but thanked her, then excused myself. Perhaps, she thought I had a secret weapon for controlling parents and children that would cause me to be a great asset to the Hooper staff. I did have a weapon—kindness. That teacher didn't know the formula for success that I had learned in my youth — "You can catch more flies with honey than with vinegar!"

9

My First P. E. Class

The morning was flowing smoothly, and it was now time for my first P.E. class of the day. While teaching my academic classes (one homeroom and two science), I was professionally dressed in slacks, shirt, tie and jacket. However, I had to change attire for the vigorous workout of a gym class. I dressed in all white — pants, sweater, socks, a cap and sneakers. The finishing touch was a whistle around my neck. Now, I looked like a coach! After the rocky start of the day, I was ready for some physical activity.

My first P.E. class consisted of 75-80 students who had to be packed into a multi-purpose classroom. (It was slightly larger than a standard size classroom, but was still no match for such a large number of students.) Uncomfortable as it was, I was determined to make it work! I was scheduled to have all classes for P.E. for at least thirty minutes, once a week, on a rotating basis. But, for now, I was on schedule and eagerly anticipating this challenge. When I walked down the hall, heading to my P.E. office, I saw one class lined up, seemingly with every eye on me. They were seventh-graders and quite anxious to get outside for what they called "recess" — a time for free play. One of the boys I had played ball with over the weekend yelled, "Hey, coach, did you bring your sneakers? We're ready for you today." With a smile, I replied, "Yes." He was dressed in full basketball apparel — headbands, armbands and kneepads. He was a funny sight! My smile was immediately erased, however, when I looked at my schedule for the next period and saw that the class size was 97! Would these challenges ever end?

As I walked past the students, I overheard some of them saying, "Boy, is he big!" My (then) 6-foot, 190-pound body frame was drawing a lot of attention, and the fact that I was black made me stand out even more! I thought, "Are they in for a surprise. There will be no playing today." I had a plan for them, and playing basketball was not on the agenda.

The first class was to be conducted in the multi-purpose room in the back of the building. I moved quickly to the room and was waiting there when the students arrived. One hundred and eight seventh-graders showed up for class along with one teacher — Ms. Catherine Cook —who served as one of the seventh-grade teachers and also coordinated music for all students. Her schedule was similar to mine, so she really didn't want to be there assisting with the supervision. Her attitude was obviously negative—she'd much rather be doing something else. Therefore, other than asking me what I wanted her to do, she didn't have anything else to say. Managing 108 students was a more pressing problem than managing a teacher with an attitude problem. I told her to come back in 25 minutes and that I could handle things alone. She looked at her watch and walked out.

The students were coming in — some a little loud, but orderly. Some would speak and others would not, which was somewhat the norm for seventh-graders. Once the last student entered the room, I blew my whistle three times for all talking to cease. Immediately, there was silence in our overcrowded classroom, and I began with a personal introduction. I went to the chalkboard and wrote my name along with class instructions such as appropriate conduct, expected participation in all activities and wearing loose-fitting attire with gym shoes. The main rule I stressed was obedience! I promised that they would learn, play, develop skills, and enjoy P.E. with me because I would plan daily activities that would be fun, yet highly organized. I informed them that Georgia law required that they each be involved in at least thirty minutes of physical education a day and explained that I would meet this expectation by having ten minutes of exercise; ten minutes of instruction on two other activities such as kickball, volleyball, softball, basketball, touch football, jogging, track relays, rope jumping, tinikling (Philippine Bird Dance), or square dancing. I'm not sure that they cared much about my rambling of Georgia law and why they needed P.E., but square dancing drew loud grousing from the students which gave me the second opportunity to blow my whistle to restore order.

After I completed my instructions, two students held their hands up, wanting permission to ask questions. The first question came from one of the young boys with whom I had played basketball. "Are we going to play basketball today?" "No, not today," I answered. He sat down, looking disappointed. The second question from a boy was twofold. "Are we going to have square dancing in P.E.? And what is tinikling?" I explained that both dances were rhythmic activities that would help young students have a well-rounded experience. Not that the little boy cared to hear the rest of my explanation, but since he asked, I felt compelled to add that these dances would help them to develop cognitive, physical, and social skills. Whether he or the rest of the students understood it or not, there were no other questions.

I could tell from some of their facial expressions that they had their reservations about me and my new approach to teaching P.E. This brief introductory process took about fifteen minutes, so for the remainder of their class time, I had them to line up in six rows of eighteen each to structure future class order. I passed a clipboard down each row for them to write down their names. Once this assignment was completed, it was time for dismissal. Ms. Cook was standing at the door, amazed at the students' good behavior and how very quiet they were. The students formed a single-file line, and as they paraded past me out of the room, some said, "See you next time."

As the seventh-graders exited, the sixth-grade teachers and students were standing outside the door waiting their turn for P.E. When they filed in, I instructed them to enter quietly and to have a seat on the floor. As they entered, I was counting each student and tallied 117! Ms. Martha Smith was the sixth-grade teacher designated to help me with supervision. She politely spoke and asked what I would need her to do. Her gesture to help seemed genuine, but I had to get a handle on this overcrowding by myself. I gave her the same instruction as I had the previous teacher. "Be back in time for dismissal." Curious, she asked what I had said to the seventh-grade class to make them act so orderly and be so quiet. I told her that all I had done was to tell them what I expected from them, stressing that obedience was a priority. The teacher wished me good luck with this class and was off to enjoy her 25-minute reprieve.

I closed the door, blew my whistle three times for order and proceeded to duplicate the instructions given to the seventh grade. This group appeared to be a little more energetic, so we began exercising sooner than I had with the seventh graders. We were organized, and the students were excited. Four of the students wanted to know more about tinikling and square dancing. Giving them my patent answer, I got the same complaint. "We don't want to do that! We want to play when we come out to P.E." I assured them that they would play, but they would learn a lot. By the time that class was over, the students' other teachers were standing at the door, looking quite stunned by the students' orderly behavior. As each teacher picked up his or her class, I heard remarks like, "If this is what P.E. is going to be like, we are going to have a great year!" Or "What a change from last year!" I thanked each of them for the kind words, but knew better than to think my problems were over. One thing that this school experience had taught me well was not to count my chickens before they hatched! Yes, things were flowing peacefully for the moment, but it was still the first day—and it wasn't over yet!

10

The Shy Little Girl

According to my schedule, it was lunchtime, and as I entered the cafeteria in my P.E. attire, I captured the attention of both teachers and students. The students were much louder than I wanted them to be so I gave a few "quiet down" gestures with my hands; they responded favorably. I passed several students as I went to get my lunch and overheard them say, "He is a real P.E. coach" and "He's very big." Many of the students had just left my P.E. classes so they were beginning to understand my expectations for their behavior. I ate my lunch in the front of the cafeteria facing the students. That way I could keep an eye on them, while at the same time being visible if anyone needed to speak to me. Little did I know that I was becoming an authority figure just by my presence. There were about ten minutes to spare between finishing my lunch and greeting my most challenging and historic class — 130 fifth-graders!

They arrived to class more excited and eager to play than the older students. Unreserved about asking questions, groups of them would come up to me posing the same question, "What are we going to play? Kickball? Baseball? Basketball? Volleyball? Relays?" Their next statements would be, "I've got my team" or "Let me pick" or "I'm first." They were an energetic bunch and having 130 of them was like having 130 firecrackers exploding at once!

I blew my whistle six times before they understood that I was signaling for them to quiet down. Their frame of reference was narrower than the upper grade students who had learned that whistle blowing meant stop all talking and unnecessary movement. Teaching them the signals for class order was one of my tasks. However, it didn't take long. After the first five minutes, I had their attention, and they were quietly sitting on the floor. Once they settled down, I noticed two students who had disabilities. They must have come in when I was trying to get control of the class and stayed close to the door.

Laurie was a little white girl with braces covering ninety percent of her body. With braces from her neck to her waist and on both arms and legs, she walked somewhat like a robot. A pretty little girl with long hair and a pleasant personality, she was quite withdrawn, and I could tell that P.E. was not one of her favorite classes. I beckoned her to come up front in order to establish total inclusion and for the other students to know that everyone would be expected to participate. Phillip, the other student, was a little white boy in a wheelchair, and I called for him to come up at the same time. When he reluctantly rolled out into the middle of the floor, I shook his hand. As with Laurie, I could tell that this was very new to him — being singled out and called up front in a P.E. class. The other students appeared somewhat stunned to see me giving this kind of recognition to disabled students, but it had grabbed their attention; they were noticeably quiet.

As with the other classes, I began with a personal introduction and class instructions. Their schedule was unique; I would see them every other day. The instruction period lasted a little longer because I wanted to make sure that they knew what I wanted them to do whether we had class inside or outside. Being typical fifth graders, I could tell they were immediately getting bored with my instructions, so I decided to line them up for exercise. I called out six names to become leaders — Laurie and Phillip, two black students (a boy and a girl), and two white students (a boy and a girl). All the other students had to get in line behind one of the line leaders. It took about five minutes to get them to stop pushing, touching each other and talking. I asked them to stand straight and to listen to my directions. I felt like a drill sergeant, but they were finally in order.

I demonstrated two exercises — jumping jacks and windmills — and had them repeat the motions. They could hardly imitate my motions for laughing uncontrollably. They were awkward and giddy. I glanced at the clock that showed it was time for their dismissal. I blew my whistle three times and they calmed down. By now, I didn't have to say a word. In one short class period, they had learned the meaning of the whistle. I knew this class was special. It was the largest, and unbeknownst to me at the time, it was going to be my greatest challenge and greatest reward.

The teachers were standing by the door, amazed that the students were orderly and quiet. I walked over and stood in the doorway to give them dismissal direction. I excused them one row at a time, allowing Laurie and Phillip to leave first and second with their lines. As the students passed by, I made remarks like, "I will see you next time" or "You did a good job today" or "Keep up the good work." Midway through the dismissal, I noticed a shy little girl with her head down and both hands around her waist with a towel covering them. She appeared nervous and kept her head down. I didn't say anything to her. Since this was her first day, I thought I would observe her and try to get to know her later.

Two days later, this energetic class came in again with the same intensity they had shown that first day. The challenge was the same—only this time, I could remind them of what I had said the last time. Shortly thereafter, they were orderly (one characteristic of fifth-graders is that they forget easily). They had lined up, with some jumping out of line, trying to get closer to a friend. My instructions were for them to stay in their positions; however, eventually, they were ready to exercise with everyone participating. We performed exercise after exercise, trying to burn off some of that energy. At the end of our class, I dismissed them the same way I had the first day, only this time I didn't notice the unusually shy little girl. Due to her class coming every other day, it had slipped my memory that I wanted to talk with her.

11

Introducing the Square Dance

The next class period, we were blessed with a beautiful day. The weather was very pleasant, so I conducted classes outside. The students and I loved being outside, not only because of the fresh air, but because there was plenty of space. My first two classes had gone extremely well, and now came the fifth grade with more energy than a jet plane. They were running and jumping and all ran up to me with the same question — "What are we going to play today?" I didn't respond, but blew my whistle and directed them to line up. They were lined up on the basketball court, and for the first time we had enough space for them to move around.

I had several planned activities — 1) basic exercises – bending and stretching; 2) jumping jacks; 3) windmills; 4) running in place; 5) tag relays; 6) rope jumping, and 7) one lap run or walk around the playground. As we began the activities, I noticed that the shy little girl, Nancy Johnson, was back with her towel or hand cloth. I couldn't focus on her because I really had to stay on top of this class. But, I noticed that she would line up fourth or fifth from the end of the line and that she kept that cloth in her hand. I didn't want to get too close because Nancy had discovered that I was conscious of her. When the class was over, she seemed to almost vanish in the crowd.

While lining them up for dismissal, I would walk by, and Nancy would be standing very straight; with her hands under the towel. Her body language practically screamed, "Don't come close." This continued for two or three weeks. By not seeing her every day, my curiosity would come and go. I thought, on a number of occasions, that she was sick and holding her stomach. I wouldn't have dared ask a little white girl who was holding her stomach what was wrong. Nevertheless, she appeared to grow more conscious of my curiosity about her. For about two weeks she would come up to me with one of the supervising teachers to say she was sick and asked to go to the library in lieu of P.E. Nancy would never come up to me by herself and seemed quite nervous each time she made this request. On occasion, I would see her going to other classes before coming out for P.E., appearing to be in fine health. Consequently, I decided that the next time she came to my P.E. class complaining of being sick and wanting to go back inside, I would request a doctor's statement explaining why she could not take P.E. class.

Wondering if she missed other classes as well, I asked one of Nancy's other 5th grade teachers, Ms. Debbie Baldwin, how she was doing in her class. To my surprise, Ms. Baldwin said she was doing fine and never gave her an ounce of trouble. I shared with her my concern about Nancy missing so many P.E. classes; so, she offered to speak to her. The next day, Ms. Baldwin informed me that the student was afraid of me. "That is not a good reason to miss her P.E. class," I replied. Obviously, something else was going on, but I couldn't figure out what it was. Ms. Baldwin agreed, yet cautioned me to be careful with Nancy because she might report me to her parents. The last thing we needed was accusations from white parents that a black teacher had intimidated their child. Maybe it was best to allow her to continue missing class rather than to create a stir with her parents. But, how could I justify excusing her (for whatever reason) when Laurie in her braces and Philip in his wheelchair participated regularly? They were my two extreme cases, and if they had no problems taking P.E., neither should anyone else!

The only other theory I could find for Nancy's lack of cooperation was her parents. I had learned that many of the white parents who decried the forced integration had told their children not to cooperate with the black teachers. Surely, this was the case with Nancy. I wasn't about to let her parents run my class! I was a teacher; Nancy was a student; and, we were there to conduct the business of education! Perhaps, the next step was a conference with Nancy's parents.

The most surprising and frightening experience of my life occurred the next day when Nancy's class came for Physical Education. They entered the room with some students complaining that they didn't want to be inside because they knew that we were going to begin the unit on square dancing. Nancy came in, easing through the crowd and looking like she hoped I wouldn't notice her. I proceeded as though I had no concern about her missed P.E. classes. Believing that I knew the cause of her behavior was her parents, my plan was already in place to call them in for a conference to straighten things out. So, until I could arrange that meeting, I wouldn't pressure her to participate. I blew my whistle for the class to get started with the regular exercise routine. They responded quickly. Nancy got in line, in her usual place, near the back of the room—second or third person from the back of the line. I stayed up front and didn't go in her direction; however, I kept a constant watch in that area to observe any abnormal behavior since she had complained about being sick. While I could not see her clearly, due to the overcrowding, I could see that she was actively participating in each exercise. When the students did hand/arm exercises, I would see a towel in one hand that was obvious, but not uncommon. A number of students had items such as headbands, armbands, sweaters around their waist, or some P.E.-related accessory.

When the exercises were over, the students had to kneel down and get as close to the wall as they could in order to leave as much space as possible for me to begin the square dance structure. I gave about a five-minute lecture on my expectations of them as participants, and when I talked about holding hands and swinging their partners, many of them muttered, "No way!" Equally as disgusting to them as holding hands was boy-girl partners! These fifth-graders were not yet romantically interested in the opposite sex, so dancing with them was the worst thing that could happen! I could barely keep a straight face without laughing at their funny statements and body language. This activity was going to be a lot of fun once we got past all of the superficial fears and discomforts. Many of them tried hiding in the crowd and surely did not want to be in the first group that would attempt to demonstrate the steps in front of their peers.

Desperate to generate interest, I tried a few psychological maneuvers. First, I told them how much the upper grades enjoyed the activity (surely, they wouldn't want to be outdone by them). When that failed to spark any interest, I shared my personal fears about learning the dance (thinking that if they knew I had fears and overcame them, that they would be more receptive to participating). That was strike two. Nothing I did seemed to make them want to learn this dance!

Russell Padget stood up and asked the question that everyone was thinking. "Mr. Edwards, do we have to touch to do this dance?" "Yes, Russell. Do you have a problem with that?" I replied. He said that he just didn't feel like touching anyone else's hand. Observing how these students enjoyed each other while exercising, I concluded that their reluctance to touch had more to do with invading their personal space than it had to do with racial differences. The boy-girl partnering was also a major bother! This class was simply going to have to adjust, because I was moving forward with this phase of my lesson plans!

Before we could enjoy the dance itself, I had to teach the class the fundamental steps. The first step I taught was "allemande left." I selected a student-partner and demonstrated the step two or three times. Laughing at my dancing relieved some of the students' anxiety. I didn't think I looked funny, but I guess that in a child's eye, a teacher dancing with a student was hilarious! It didn't matter that they were laughing, because they were paying attention and learning the steps! At times, they cackled so loudly that I blew the whistle to restore order.

The second step I taught was "swing your partner." I selected a different student-partner who was just as comfortable dancing with me as her classmate. It was becoming clear that the racial barriers were coming down (or were not even there for students this age).

Children are not born with prejudices, they are taught them. If parents (and other adults) don't pollute their minds with hatred and bitterness for people who are different from themselves, children could make monumental strides in establishing racial harmony.

Sufficient for today was my teaching them to square dance. Maybe this activity would be the catalyst for these students to promote change in their lifetime. I could only hope and pray that the impact would be that far-reaching. After I had demonstrated my dance steps, I asked the class to give the students a round of applause for their participation. Everyone clapped enthusiastically! Class time was over, and I felt that they were ready for their first dance lesson. The next class would be the test.

When the bell rang, signaling dismissal, the students were relieved that they didn't have to dance with each other that day. It would have been fine with them if I had demonstrated the entire square dance sequence while they watched. It wasn't as much the activity itself as it was the touching that was involved with it! As usual, I stood at the door as the students filed out of class in a singular line. Nancy passed by with her hands around her waist tucked under a towel. Touching her on the shoulder to get her to halt, I asked her if she was still sick.

She stopped walking and responded affirmatively. I told her to bring me a note from her parents and a doctor stating that she couldn't participate in P.E. class. Holding her head down and looking at the floor, she softly answered, "Yes sir." Sensing her discomfort with me, I told her that she could give the note to her homeroom teacher. Having nothing else to say, Nancy left. As the other students filed out saying goodbye and chatting among themselves, I was glad that they saw me stop Nancy to talk to her. In case my touching her on the shoulder ever came back to haunt me, I had witnesses that it was a touch to simply get her attention as she was leaving class. It was not a push or a hit, just a touch. With racial tension as heated as it was at the time, any touch could be misconstrued and blown out of proportion! All I wanted to do was make a positive impact on a student who appeared to lack self-confidence and seemed unhappy.

As I sat home that evening, thinking about the next time I would see Nancy's class, I plotted an idea to get her involved. I decided that if she had more responsibility in class, she would want to come regularly and participate. My plan was to give her a leadership role, and square dancing was the perfect opportunity! She could be a group leader! Yes, what an ingenious plan! I couldn't wait to execute it!

12

Discovering Nancy's Secret

On her next scheduled P.E. day, Nancy entered the class, rushing past me without uttering a word. Trying to break the ice, I complimented her on the pretty blue dress she was wearing. She thanked me as she continued walking to her usual spot in the back of the room. Little did she know that I had a master plan for her that day! As with the start of every class, we began with a few warm-up exercises. Occasionally, I glanced over in her direction to see if she was participating. She was aware that I was watching her and dared not draw any undue attention to herself by not participating. When the warm-ups were over, she moved to the other side of the room where a larger number of students were gathered (it was easier for her to get lost in the crowd that way). Nothing she could do that day could make her invisible to me. I was on a mission, and there was no escape for Nancy Johnson!

Pairing the students as partners was the preparation phase of square dancing. I carefully paired students, taking into account their size and height. Clipboard in hand, I called names and positioned students in the room to form small squares. The first two students chosen were a black boy and a white girl. They came to the center of the room, and I placed them in position. As I called other students to the middle of the room, they screamed, "No way" and "Oh no!" referring to their partners. The next five students were three white boys, a white girl and a black girl. This was group number one. Their formation was complete. The next six groups offered resistance, but complied. I didn't have much tolerance for horseplay because I had to pair up 130 students! The process alone took up half the class period! As much as they fussed, I could tell that the students were enjoying the process. All except Nancy. As more students were paired and positioned in their square, there were fewer students for her to hide behind.

The next set of names to be called would include Nancy's. I called hers last, and she refused to come out. I repeated her name, and still she did not come forth. Her action silenced the class because this had not happened before.

Though many complained, no one refused. Suddenly she shouted, "I'm not going to do it!" and walked toward the door to leave. Losing my composure, I yelled back, "Yes you are!" Having never seen this side of me, the other students whispered, "She's in trouble now! She'd better get in line!" They were right in assuming that this situation was heating up! I wasn't tolerating belligerent behavior from Nancy—especially since I had skillfully planned a way to include her in the class! I walked over to her and sternly said, "Little girl, you are going to get in line just like everybody else!" We were standing face-to-face as Nancy yelled at the top of her lungs, "I'm not going to do it!" "Yes, you are!" I ordered. I think I had thrown my clipboard on the floor in my anger. I continued, "If you are going to stay in this class, you are going to participate!" I expected her to continue her volatile debate with me, but she threw me a curve. Instead of yelling back at me, she stood there shaking and crying uncontrollably. Had I pushed this child over the edge? This was not part of my ingenious plan! Things were falling apart, and I didn't know what to do. Thank goodness the other children were scared motionless, because I couldn't deal with Nancy and a mob of fifth-graders!

As Nancy looked at me with tear-filled eyes, I knew her fear was not square dancing. In fact, I became a little fearful of what the actual problem could be. Boy, they had not covered this situation in any textbook! For a few moments, neither of us spoke. Perhaps, we were exhausted from our outburst. Nancy cried, and I stood there searching for answers. Fearlessly, Nancy walked toward the door to leave class. Compassionately, I walked with her placing my hand on her shoulder. Before we reached the door, I walked ahead and faced her to ask, "Nancy, why are you so upset? Are you afraid of me?" In the midst of her sobbing she said, "No." I knelt on the floor, gently guiding her to do likewise. With both of us sitting on the floor, I guess I looked less threatening. My plan was not to threaten, but to understand what was wrong with my student. She sat with her head lowered, and I asked what could be so dreadfully wrong that she wouldn't participate in class. Slowly, she unwrapped the towel from her hands and raised them in front of my face. The problem was abundantly clear—she had no fingers!

Vestiges of fingers were in the place of her "little" fingers and her thumbs. Nubs, no longer than knuckles, branched out in the middle of her small hands. She had tears streaming down her face as she anticipated my reaction (more accurately, my rejection) to her dark secret. Though the class was a reasonable distance away from us, she had exposed herself to everyone, risking embarrassment and shame. When she looked at me, her soul seemed to cry out, "Please help me! Don't turn me away. Please help me!"

Momentarily, I was stunned and frightened. I had never seen anything like this and wasn't sure how to handle the situation, but I knew I had to handle it! Disappointing this little girl was not an option, and I was determined to respond to her cry for help. How frightening it must have been for her to unwrap that towel and expose her hands to me. It took courage. Now it was my turn to show courage in a frightening situation. My first instinct was to hug her; then I realized that she might interpret that as pity, and she certainly didn't need any of that! More importantly, she needed strength and support, but where was I to get it? As with every challenge I had met thus far, I prayed about it and, within seconds, something supernatural consumed me, wiping away all fear and worry. From that point on, I did not concern myself with our racial or gender differences or even the racist behavior shown to me by some staff members and parents. I began to see Nancy as God meant for us to see each other—as human beings interdependent upon one another. I saw Nancy's need and promised to help her find self-confidence and to dream with hope—hope of becoming a productive person rather than a product of fear and shame. A burning desire to reach out and to help this student in a way that no one had ever done before consumed me. As I stood in front of her with these thoughts and feelings racing through me a mile a minute, I could sense her anticipation of rejection. I had not made a move since she showed me her hands. I experienced a range of emotions, but I had not reacted to Nancy. Surely, she was waiting for a groan, frown or other sign of disapproval from me, but she wasn't going to get it!

Looking into Nancy's eyes, I gently said, "Give me your towel and trust me. I will help you overcome this problem, but you will have to help me do so, and together we can do anything! One thing you must accept is that we can't do anything about your fingers. That will never change, but what I can help you with is to be the best you can be with what you have! You can learn square dancing and lots of other things without fingers. Let's work together, and you'll see." I put her towel in my back pocket, took her by the hand, and said, "Come, let's go to your position in the square." We both stood up and walked back, hand-in-hand, to rejoin the class.

I was amazed at how quiet the class had been during my conference with Nancy. They hadn't seen her hands, so obviously they were not responding to that. Perhaps, they were confused by my behavior, which had drastically shifted from aggressive to docile. They didn't know what had transpired between Nancy and me and were too afraid to step out-of-line for fear of setting off my temper again. I took Nancy to her assigned group and positioned her in the square. Her classmates clapped to see her participating even though they were still oblivious to the reason for her shyness.

The tone in the class had shifted from giddiness to seriousness. As I resumed calling out the remaining students to form squares, no one else complained or grumbled about their partners. By the time all fourteen groups had formed, only ten minutes of class time remained. That was enough time for me to teach one or two steps.

Using my previous strategy of letting the disabled students lead (to include them in the group), I called Nancy's group to the middle of the floor to demonstrate the steps. I wanted Nancy to be a part of the activity from the onset and to feel comfortable with participating. It had worked with Laurie and Philip, so why not her? Still requiring a little prodding, Nancy walked with her group to the designated area. She glanced at me as if to say, "I'm trusting you. Don't let me down." I had no reservations about my decision. In fact, I was so confident that it was the right thing to do that I stood back to watch this scene play itself out perfectly—sort of like flying a plane then putting it on automatic pilot. I knew it would stay on course. The charted course would lead to acceptance, and the sooner I engaged her in this activity, the sooner she would experience acceptance from classmates, then ultimately herself.

Nancy and her partner took the lead position as she stood with tears welling in her eyes. She was striving to be courageous in the midst of fear of disapproval from classmates. The first step — "allemande left" — required each student to face his or her opposite partner; raise the left hand almost head- high; walk toward the opposite partner; join left hands in the air; walk in a circle for four steps; then return to his or her original partner. Before the group started, I demonstrated this maneuver with a student from a different group. As usual, the class could hardly stop themselves from laughing at my dancing with a student. The levity was much needed.

Blowing my whistle to restore order, it was time for Nancy's group to perform. When Nancy turned to face her opposite partner, raising her hand head-high and reaching to join hands with him, her worst fear became reality. The little boy yelled, "Look at that hand! No fingers! Don't touched me with that thing!" The majority of the class began laughing and teasing her. Quickly, she retracted her hands, tucked them under her clothes and ran to the door crying uncontrollably.

The strategy, which had worked so perfectly for Laurie and Philip, had failed for Nancy. The class was more accepting of the students in body braces and a wheelchair than they were of Nancy with missing fingers. The major difference was that Laurie's and Philip's physical appearance was not disfigured. I had not factored that difference into my strategy.

I rushed to the door to prevent Nancy from leaving the room, although I completely understood her need to escape. I didn't say anything, but grabbed her gently by the shoulders to stop her from leaving. She seemed too exhausted to offer resistance. Not struggling, she simply cried, "Let me go. Please just let me go!" I threw my arms around her and hugged her tightly as if trying to absorb her pain. "Nancy, listen to me! Just listen!" I pleaded. Turning toward the class, I blew my whistle to restore order. Nancy was again squirming, unsuccessfully, to break free from my arms. There were two major situations going on here: Nancy, and the class! Both had to be dealt with immediately, but class time was running out!

13

The After-Shock –
Teaching and Preaching

Nancy and I both were faced with our worst fears: for her, rejection and ridicule from classmates about a condition that she could not control; for me, helping her to jump a hurdle that was difficult to jump and impossible to remove. But, I was determined to help her jump it in any way I could. At the moment, a good starting place was Nancy's fifth-grade Physical Education class! I relaxed my grip on Nancy when she stopped struggling to break away, but she clung tightly to my leg. I walked back to rejoin the class with Nancy dragging along. I took her to my desk and sat her in my chair. She laid her head on the desk and continued crying and uttering, "I want to go. I just want to go."

Turning to the class in exasperation, I ordered them to dismantle their squares and to be seated on the floor, forming a large circle. For the last five minutes of class, they were in store for the "chewing out" of their lives! How dare they mock and tease a classmate! I reprimanded them for their callous behavior and told them that I would not tolerate it again! I asked them what they thought their parents would think of their behaviors. Though I knew that I could not change their attitudes in one day, I could correct heartless behavior! Before leaving class, they had to apologize to Nancy. I directed all of them to stand and say, "Nancy, we're sorry, and this won't happen again."

At that time, one of their teachers opened the door to see what was going on since I had detained the students five minutes past dismissal time. Ms. Baldwin could detect that something was wrong. She didn't ask any questions about the situation, but, instead, asked if we needed a little more time. I'm sure the students were ready to go, but they had not yet experienced the full wrath of Lonnie Edwards! I accepted Ms. Baldwin's offer to keep them a few additional minutes and asked if she would check with the other classroom teachers to ask if they also wouldn't mind. The teachers agreed that I could retain the students twenty more minutes. That was perfect! The next hour was my planning period, so no other classes were waiting for them to exit. The few students who had started to get up from the circle in preparation to leave had now resumed sitting, awaiting phase two of their scolding. To the contrary, I used the time to teach valuable lessons in acceptance, love and respect. My role had changed from disciplinarian to humanitarian.

I spent three to five minutes each on four topics. I started with "self-acceptance," teaching them to be proud of themselves whether they were black, white, yellow, brown, fat, skinny, short or tall. I told them that God made us the way He wanted us—with differences included—and not to let anyone make them feel bad because they might not be like the majority of the people. Incorporating Nancy's situation, I pointed out that God gave some of us ten fingers and others received more or less. Regardless of our condition, we must learn to like ourselves and work at being successful. I glanced at Nancy out of the corner of my eye and could see that she was no longer slumped over on the desk crying. I'm sure she was still hurt from her experience, but she seemed to be paying attention to me.

My next topic was "accepting others." By encouraging them to take a good look at themselves, they would start to see others differently. I reminded them of the Golden Rule: "Do unto others as you would have them do unto you." We will experience many differences in our lives, but we must learn to work, play and live together. This meant supporting and loving each other even when we are different.

I shared my college experience at Montevallo as one of a few black students in a predominately white school. It was difficult adjusting to people who didn't like me just because my skin color was different, but I "hung in there" because I had no control over being black. However, I could control my behavior and attitudes, and eventually, I gained the respect of my classmates by not acting like them! I made my students repeat three times, "You are what you are and who you are because God made you" and, "No matter what others say, I will always be proud of who I am." I told them that I wanted them to love themselves like I loved myself. With that, I gave myself a big hug exclaiming, "I love me!" They laughed at my gesture, thinking it was corny, I'm sure. Looking at Nancy briefly, she too had a smile on her face. I knew the lesson was sinking in.

"Loving others as friends," was the next lesson. I encouraged them to believe that nothing was better in the world than for them to love and treat each other as friends, including people with disabilities. I beckoned Laurie, Philip and Nancy to the floor. Reluctantly, they joined me in the middle of the room. I could sense their uneasiness with being brought "center stage," but it was necessary to illustrate the point. I faced the three of them and affirmed, "We are going to love you like you are going to love us. I will teach you how." I sent them back to their places, and I could see all of them give a big sigh of relief. The students were smiling at each other and at me. Looking at their reactions, I was confident that positive changes would result from our lessons.

The final lesson in my 20-minute lecture was "Never hurt each other." In this topic, I had to expand their awareness of "hurt" since their frame-of-reference for this term was limited to physical pain. It didn't take long for me to broaden it for them, using examples like "saying bad things to someone" or "criticizing others" causes pain, too. That kind of pain makes people feel sad and depressed. We promised to not let that kind of behavior occur in our class. If one of them witnessed another student saying hurtful comments to another, he/she would ask the person to stop. If the student continued, he/she would be reported to me for disciplinary action.

My overtime was up, and students had to go to their next class. I took my usual position at the door to watch the students file out singularly. When Nancy passed, I asked her if things were all right. She smiled, and softly said, "Yes sir." Her hands were still tucked underneath her blouse, and it occurred to me that in all the ruckus, I had never returned her towel (which was still in my back pocket). As she walked down the hall, she held her head low. After all the students had left the multi-purpose room, I walked down the hall to keep an eye on Nancy. I was sure it wouldn't take long for the "fifth grade grapevine" to spread the news of our class ordeal. I didn't want other students teasing her since her well-kept secret was now out in the open. In fact, I felt responsible for what had happened. Sooner or later students would have learned about her deformed hands, but since I had made it happen sooner than later, I had to protect her.

I continued to follow her at a distance until she entered her classroom. I even stood in the hall an extra few minutes to see if she would request permission to leave. It was the last period of the day, and I thought that she might want to leave ahead of the other students to avoid any hecklers.

I spent my planning time processing what had occurred in class and anticipating what was next. Surely, I could be Nancy's protector in P.E. class, but students who meant her harm would find other opportunities to harass her. I needed a plan. While I was trying to think of one, other thoughts popped into my head. "What would Nancy tell her parents about what had happened in class?" "What would other students tell their parents?" "Would Mr. Christopher find out or should I tell him?" Again, there were no textbook answers for these questions. And, "What about the fact that I had embraced this student?" A black teacher touching a white student was unheard of, but hugging one was surely forbidden! Well, I certainly couldn't undo what had already been done. So, if there were repercussions for my actions, I would have to face them! Mr. Christopher was bound to find out that something out of the ordinary had occurred in my class that day because I detained students from four teachers! All those worries had to wait their turn. For the moment, I could only think of Nancy and what she was feeling.

With twenty minutes left in the school day, I could not resist going by Nancy's class to peep in the door to see if she was still there. She was sitting in the back of the class, three chairs from the last. The two black students sitting behind her were experiencing social adjustment problems, but their woes were no match for Nancy's. For them, social acceptance would occur faster than acceptance of Nancy's physical deformity. While I stared at her, Nancy never looked up as she was leaning over the desk busily writing.

I stepped away from the door feeling relieved that she stayed in class and didn't attempt to sneak out early. To me, this was a small victory, as I thought about all that could or would have happened to a black teacher who did what I had just done. As I recalled, the most devastating thing about this matter was that I didn't have anybody at Hooper that I could truly trust to help counsel me with this very sensitive matter.

However, the more I thought about it, the more I convinced myself that I needed to take this incident to Mr. Christopher before he heard about it and brought it to me. If I took it to him, I could explain; if he came to me, I would have to defend my actions. Having had my share of battles since joining this staff, my first choice seemed to be the lesser of two evils. I went to his office requesting about five minutes of his time. He listened, asking the child's name and writing it on his notepad. When asked if I had put my hands on her, I said,

"Yes sir." With no details of the "whens" or "whys," he scolded, "Don't do that anymore because it may be very difficult to explain that to an angry parent with a dissatisfied student." I responded, "Yes sir," trying to describe the nature of the touch and that everything had occurred in the presence of the class. He said he would just wait and see what happened; he would talk with Nancy's parents, if he needed to. I thanked him for listening, and as I was exiting the office, Mr. Christopher added, "By the way, let me make a suggestion. Don't ever keep the class for two periods anymore because it takes them off of their regularly-scheduled activities." Of course, he knew of the situation and was waiting to see if I came forth to explain! Boy, was I elated with my decision to go to him first! I responded, "Yes sir" and tried again to explain why I had done so. He didn't appear concerned with the details. However, since I wasn't sure exactly what he had been told and by whom, it was important for me to set the record straight so he wouldn't think something awful had happened. Nevertheless, my attempts to enlighten him were futile. He shrugged me off by saying that he understood that I could have a good reason, but in the future there would be no good reason unless he gave it to me! Thinking that my reprimand could have been worse than this verbal "slap-on-the-wrist," I meekly promised it wouldn't happen again.

Reflecting on my conversation with Mr. Christopher, I felt disappointed because he had offered no advice on how I should have handled the matter, but was quick to reprimand me. In fact, he never allowed me to fully explain the incident. Also, I thought, "Why did a teacher or teachers report me to the Principal when they agreed that I could keep the students for an extended amount of time?" This puzzling question made me want to confront the four teachers involved to learn who had squealed! Reluctantly, I refrained from asking, realizing that it wouldn't solve the problem at hand anyway.

Nancy had experienced a traumatic moment in my class, and though I attempted to deal with it, the success (or failure) of my intervention was yet to be seen. I wondered, "Had I gained her trust? Did the class learn to accept people regardless of differences? Would students tease her outside of class? And, how many other students knew about her now that I had exposed her?" Only time could answer these questions.

My grueling workday came to a close around 4:30 p.m. En route to my car, I met the four boys with whom I had previously played basketball, and they were begging me to play at least one game. Needing a physical release, I agreed to play a game. As I put my books in the car, one of the little boys said, "Mr. Edwards, who was that little fifth-grade girl that you took a towel from that had no fingers on either hand?" That stunned me because he was in the seventh grade! I knew the fifth-graders would get the word out among their peers, but I had no idea that the news had reached the upper grades so quickly! I asked him how he knew about it, and he told me that he had heard it in the neighborhood from some of the children talking about it. I asked what they were saying. The young boy said, "Oh, nothing. That you made her do what the other children were doing in square dancing, and she started crying a lot, and you stopped and started talking to all of them about helping her to be like everybody else." I polled the other three boys for their opinions of the situation but they had no comments. The fourth boy spoke up and said, "She should have at least tried, and maybe she would learn how to fit in and not be ashamed of her condition." That was a great answer, and I hoped that everyone else shared his sentiment!

We played two games with my team being victorious in both. My competitors were happy that I played with them, but disappointed that they lost. I think these boys were delighted to spend time with me; winning was secondary. It certainly was for me! They could not match my playing skill, but this day they had been a great source of therapy! Playing ball with them was the highlight of my day, yet I was extremely concerned about my career. The news of what had happened to Nancy was already spreading through the community, and these people had a short fuse for racial matters. Even though our encounter was not racially motivated, it would become a racial issue by virtue of Nancy being white and my being black. I bid the boys good-bye, got in my car and headed for home. Along the way, all I could think about was what I could have done differently instead of getting involved with Nancy and now having to worry about everybody — the Principal, parents, teachers and students. This was much more than I had expected, so I thought maybe the best thing to do was to draft a letter of resignation.

14

Faith Conquers Fears

I spent the better part of my evening trying to relax and to plan my next course of action. After much soul-searching and contemplation, I was confident that I had done the right thing with Nancy and the class. The more I thought about what had happened, the better I began to feel, knowing that I had confronted a student with low self-esteem and challenged her and her peers to learn acceptance (of self and others). Finding voids and filling them is the ultimate challenge of teaching! Nancy had presented that challenge — I had accepted!

I knelt down to pray and couldn't get past my request ... "Lord, please help me to master this problem; to help Nancy and the other children understand the real value of love for each other." Also, I asked that God give me the courage and knowledge to withstand any confrontations surrounding this problem. Finishing that prayer, I drifted off to sleep. That was the most restless night of my life. I awakened ten to twenty times, receiving a new reflection each time. "Resign. Let them have this job. They don't want you there anyway," were my own thoughts. Words of wisdom from significant people in my life crept in. My grandmother's words flashed before me. "If you are right and not wrong, God will stand with you, and you will never be alone." My mother's input was, "When times get tough, stick your chest out and be tough." My Uncle James's words were, "Hang on in there anyhow, because trouble won't last always," and "Behind every dark cloud, the sun will shine." I could hear my Aunt Bertha say, "Don't give up. Stay in there and fight because the game of life will give you a tough blow at times, but if you stay in there, it will lighten up and the experience from that blow will help you in the next fight."

Sunday School Bible verses that had stayed with me from the time I was a young boy, began racing through my mind .... "If God be for you who can be against you?"...... "Acknowledge Him in all thy ways and He will direct your path."...... "Whatever you want from God, ask in faith and He will grant it in grace."

I saw flashbacks of my University of Montevallo days when hate and racism were rampant. I recalled the dusty, dark evening I left the cafeteria on my way to the dormitory when I saw a noose hanging out of a tree — a death signal that someone had left for me. And, I thought of the night a group of students poured gasoline around my dormitory room door, starting a fire; I opened a window for ventilation because I feared leaving my room. Through these and many other frightening experiences, I stuck it out and graduated on time. I had faced challenges before with faith, courage and inspirational words from loved ones, and I could do it again!

How could I possibly entertain the thought of resigning because of the Hooper experience? I had survived far worse than gossipy teachers, demanding bosses, irate parents and angry community members. Compared to the Montevallo experience, this should be a *"cake walk in the park!"* I had to stick this out; not only for myself, but for Nancy. This challenge was different. A human being — a little girl with a disability — was yearning for help; for a way out of deep state of loneliness and suffering from being a social outcast.

By this time, I had turned over and was looking out the window at the dawn of a new day. I was so glad to see the light that I leaped out of the bed, knelt down and prayed, "Lord, thank you for letting me get up this morning. Please give me strength to challenge this day and help me to manage my problems on my job. Help me to help the children to be the best that they can be." I got dressed, ate a quick breakfast and headed to work thirty minutes earlier than usual. I suppose I was anticipating a day of confrontations and of justifying my actions from the previous day.

15

Waiting for the Showdown

I reached the Hooper campus in fifteen minutes, and when I walked in the building, no one was there except the Principal and Custodian. Mr. Christopher commented that I was there mighty early that morning. I responded, "Yes sir, I had a pretty long night worrying about my problem." He told me that he had given it a little more thought, but doubted I would have any major problems from the incident. He suggested we just "play it by ear," and if I needed him, he would be there to help me like I had helped him the first day of school. His gesture of support was much better than it was the day before when all he did was scold me. He added, "I can't thank you enough and believe me, Mr. Edwards, we are in this together." I couldn't believe my ears! I thanked him for his support and went to my classroom. Prayer and one night made a difference in Mr. Christopher's attitude and behavior. Surely, the results would extend into my workday and the demands it had in store.

The day had started off on a positive note, and now, I was waiting on Nancy's parents. No one had said that they were coming, but surely, they would come once Nancy reported the news about our encounter in class. While sitting at my desk, I tried to review the day's lesson, but I wasn't successful. My mind drifted to what I would say to Nancy's parents. Would an apology be appropriate? But, I hadn't done anything wrong! Would they come in my room yelling or screaming or would they be grateful that I tried to help their daughter gain self-respect and acceptance? There was no way to predict this scene or rehearse my lines; so, I walked to the doorway and stood there. At least, I would be able to see them coming down the hall, and maybe I could ascertain their mood before they entered my room.

Teachers and students began entering the building and going to their classrooms. About five minutes before the bell rang for everybody to be in class, I saw Nancy enter the hallway on her way to class and knew that she would soon pass my door. My heart began to beat faster as I sweated and braced myself for her parents to turn the corner at any second. Nancy turned the corner; she was alone. She had books in her arms and a little bookbag was hanging on her shoulder. She looked at me, and I said, "Good morning, Nancy." Smiling, she said, "Good morning." Nancy never slowed her pace in walking and continued to class after our brief greeting. I stood there watching her until she entered her classroom. I felt so relieved after seeing and speaking to her (without her parents) that I could hardly contain myself.

I rushed to the Principal's office and peeked in; no one was there. My sweating stopped for a moment and everything began to feel normal. Returning to my class with a smile, I couldn't recall when I had felt any better. When I walked into the room, the students spoke in chorus, "Good morning, Mr. Edwards." I greeted them back with a hardy, "Good morning!" and began calling the class roll while listening for, and still expecting to hear, a knock at my door. About five minutes later, that knock came. Mr. Christopher was standing at the door. I rushed over to open it, and there stood a new black student with her parents. Mr. Christopher introduced me to them before leaving them with me. We shook hands, and the father said, "We are glad to meet you. We have already heard a lot of good things about you." I thanked him and promised to be available to help them if I could. We shook hands again as he departed, and I took the student into the room, introduced her to the class, gave her a seat and began the lesson with my reading class. That father left thinking that I was the most friendly teacher he had ever met. Little did he know that I was shaking his hand out of relief that he wasn't Nancy's parents! So far, things had gone much better than I had anticipated.

About 11:15 a.m., the bell rang signaling the end of my morning academic classes. I rushed to my office to change clothes and to get ready for the afternoon P.E. classes. This day, my lesson plans had changed. Instead of teaching square dance to the seventh-graders, I was going to give them about ten minutes of exercise and proceed to the lecture that I had given the fifth-graders the previous day on accepting and loving others. It was obvious to the students that I was in a "no-nonsense" mood. I directed them to have a seat on the floor and to give me their undivided attention because I had something extremely important to talk to them about.

One of the students, a white boy named Jeff Babb whose mother was a member of the PTA, raised his hand and asked if they had done anything wrong or was this related to what had happened in the fifth grade the day before. I asked him what he knew about that situation with the fifth-grade P.E. class. He told me that his sister, Deborah, a sixth-grader, had told them about "a girl who had no fingers and that you had made her try to learn how to square dance, and the girl got real upset and that you had taken her towel."

I confirmed the truth about the girl and my attempt to get her involved with the other students. But, I let them know that her crying was not an intentional move on my part. Knowing that the news about Nancy was spreading through the student body in the usual fashion that gossip does—erroneously—I was convinced that this lecture was necessary for every student in the building!

These were seventh-graders, and a number of them were already experiencing the realities of differences and diversity. So, this discussion was a timely one with or without the Nancy saga. "Mr. Edwards, who is Nancy Johnson?" and "Is it true that she does not have any fingers?", two students asked. I told them it was true and jumped right into the lecture on self-acceptance; acceptance of others; loving each other as friends; never hurting each other; and not putting down their peers by saying negative or critical things about them because they were different in some way......be it race, color, size, economics, or disability which included Nancy and others with obvious differences.

During this fifteen-minute lecture period, the students didn't say a word. They appeared to be stunned by my compassion for them and my interest in their treating each other with respect. My closing remark to them that day was, "When each of you leaves today, I want you to think about caring about one another and loving each other because I love you, and I want you to help me to help you and people like Nancy." By then, our time was up, and I directed them to get in line for dismissal. You could have heard a pin fall. One of the teachers, Ms. Coley, opened the door, observed their behavior and asked me, quietly, what they had done—implying that their orderliness was in response to a reprimand. I explained that they hadn't done anything; that we were just trying to get a better understanding about life. She commented that they had never been that quiet leaving a P.E. class. Before we could say more, the sixth-graders began approaching the door, and we had to end our conversation.

As the sixth-graders filed into the room, I overheard one of them ask a seventh-grader who was leaving what they had done in class. The student simply said, "Mr. Edwards talked a lot." Little did they know they had the same agenda coming, and when their class period was over, they left feeling the same way.

Later that day, the fourth-graders got the same lecture, and they too responded like the other classes—calmly and pensively. Grades one through three were spared the lecture. We had fun running, jumping, exercising and playing kickball.

At the end of the day, word had gotten around that I had done more preaching than teaching to my P.E. classes, and it was because of that little girl without fingers. I stayed around school late that day—particularly near the Principal's office— waiting to see if Nancy's parents were coming.

Around 4:15 p.m., I left the building heading for home. I felt great! Nancy's parents hadn't come to school for a "showdown," and I had delivered my inspirational message to all the students. I was proud of myself and believed that another day of that kind of teaching (or preaching) would set the stage for me to continue my square dance lessons.

16

Still Teaching and Preaching

The next morning, I arrived early, still expecting to meet Nancy's parents. I signed in around 7:40 a.m. and was greeted by Mr. Christopher. I asked if he had heard anything concerning Nancy. He said that he hadn't, but that he had heard about me and my preaching. I expected a verbal warning for this, but to my surprise, he smiled and said, "Keep up the good work."

About 8:05 a.m., I saw Nancy coming up the hall, heading for her class. As she passed my door, she spoke first and said, "Good morning." I replied, "Good morning. How are you?" She smiled and said she was fine, yet, from my observation, still very shy and withdrawn. Even so, she had made my morning, and I was off to a good start for the day.

I could hardly wait for my P.E. classes because I knew that Nancy's class was scheduled to have P.E.; I wanted to observe and review the attitudes of the students. I conducted class the same way that I had two days before, with one exception — I asked questions about what I had tried to teach and share with them. Surprisingly, a number of hands went up with answers, and after listening to their responses, I was thoroughly impressed with their comprehension level. I drew the same conclusion from each class. However, one of the fifth-grade boys stopped on his way out of the door and asked me if they were ever going to do anything other than exercise and listen to me talk. I smiled and promised that we would do other things.

At the end of that day, I left school feeling as though I had really made an impact on the majority of the students. Another consoling point was that I still hadn't heard from Nancy's parents. I was beginning to believe that I was on target with what was needed to help the students in the area of social development.

17

Picking Up Where We Left Off

The next day, I returned with vigor, ready to resume square dancing with each class. I was unusually upbeat that morning; having fun with students as they walked into the room. The students seemed happier with the fact that I was smiling, and they began saying, one to another, "Mr. Edwards is happy about something." I overheard one make the statement, "I sure hope Mr. Edwards is that way when we get to P.E. because I am ready to have some fun when we go out to play. Please, you all, let's not make him upset about anything because we don't want a preaching today." I ignored them, but I got the message; I was tired of the lecturing, too.

The first two periods went smoothly with everything running like clockwork. Finally, the bell sounded for me to get ready for my P.E. classes; the students were curious to see what was going to happen. I rushed to re-dress and headed for the P.E. room. I moved things around a bit, took out the record player and got ready for square dancing. By now, the seventh grade was coming in the room and lining up for exercise without my instruction. The row leaders were on their jobs. All that I had to do was call out the exercise, and they would begin carrying out the routine. I thought to myself that they truly must have been fed up with my talking and weren't going to risk having me repeat that episode of instructions.

After ten minutes of exercise, I called groups one through four out onto the floor to walk through a dance routine. This went so smoothly that they were only on the floor for five minutes. Groups five through eight and the remainder of the groups responded the same way. The last seven or eight minutes, I directed three groups to demonstrate the routines with music and encouraged everyone to participate by quietly clapping their hands. This was so much fun that they didn't want to leave. Many of them were now singing the words and trying to do a step or two. They appeared to love the "do-si-do" dance step. At dismissal time, they were not ready to go. After blowing my whistle two or three times for order, they finally calmed down, and on their way out the door, all I heard was,

"Goodbye, Mr. Edwards, I'll see you tomorrow. We had a good time." Standing there in the doorway, I smiled at each of them and said I would see them tomorrow.

The sixth-graders were now standing at the door, in single file, listening to what the seventh graders were saying. When they entered the room, they prepared for exercises — almost exactly duplicating what had just happened with the seventh-graders. I conducted their class the same as I had the seventh-graders and got the same results. At dismissal time, I got the same response. This was almost too good to be true! I hated to break for lunch because things were going just that well! I hurried to get a quick lunch and went back to the P.E. room to get ready for Nancy and the fifth-graders.

18

The Dance of Courage

I could almost tell that something miraculous was getting ready to happen, but I wasn't sure of what to expect from this fifth-grade group. To my surprise, they entered the room almost exactly like grades six and seven. I directed them to begin with exercises, and they were almost perfect for fifth-graders.

Now came the BIG announcement, "We are going to square dance." When I directed them to have a seat around the wall as close as they could, I received full cooperation from the class. The room became unusually quiet.

I walked out into the middle of the floor and called for Nancy to come out and join me in demonstrating the steps that we were going to learn that day. She reluctantly walked out with her arms folded and head somewhat bowed, but nowhere near what it was like the first time she came out to take her place in the square. Our first sequence was "allemande left." I turned and faced Nancy. I directed her to stand up straight, raise her left hand, take two steps in my direction, and put her hand in mine. She slowly raised her hand as if anticipating rejection. Her hand touched mine, and we circled around four steps. When she saw she was not being rejected, she was ecstatic! Her eyes gazed directly into my face with a stare that I shall never forget. A glow covered her little face, and she couldn't contain herself. She was trembling so badly that I grabbed both of her hands and said, "Nancy, Nancy, you were great." Then, I directed the class to give her a round of applause. She calmed down somewhat, but never lost contact with my eyes. I could only imagine what was going on inside of her head. With a show of courage, she had met triumph; her tribulation was over. At last, she had touched someone, besides her family members, who did not reject her. I was so touched by this thought that tears came up in my eyes, and I wanted to openly cry. But, instead, I started to chant — "Nancy-Nancy-Nancy" — and the entire class joined in. This chanting lasted about half a minute, and by that time, Nancy was openly clapping her hands with a grin on her face that I thought could last forever. I directed the class to cease the chanting, but Nancy seemingly couldn't stop clapping, so the chanting started again — "Nancy-

Nancy-Nancy" — for another half minute. For the second time, I directed them to stop the clapping. Nancy was smiling. She was finally free from the many years of hiding and trying to cover up reality. And, for me, and the entire class, what a triumph! We had grown to another level.

After such a grand victory, we continued the demonstration of other routines. The next step was "swing your partner" which drew a loud response from the students. I gave them my stare, and they quickly calmed down. They were laughing because when I took Nancy's hand and put my other hand on her shoulder, I had had to lean over so she could touch my shoulder; that was funny to them. We completed that routine. The next step was the "right and left grand." We walked through an imaginary circle until we met each other. The next step was the "promenade." Nancy was becoming more comfortable with what was happening, and so were the other students.

I called the remainder of Nancy's group out onto the floor and stepped out of the circle to see how things would go without me. They repeated the routine that Nancy and I had demonstrated. To my delight, Nancy had become an expert and was giving directions to her partner along with other members of the group. They responded very well, and we had a complete group. I had the other students give that group a hardy round of applause. Dismissal time came quickly, and as they began to line up to exit the room, Nancy walked over, hugged my leg and said, "Thank you, Mr. Edwards, I had fun." And then, her questions began — "Can I stay and show the next class how to square dance?" I responded, "No." "Can I come tomorrow?" I said, "No." Then, she said, "Well, I will see you next time." She left the room with a sway in her walk. I had never witnessed so much pride in anybody, and never was I any happier.

After everyone had left, I closed the door; walked around in the room and thanked God for what had happened because I was convinced that a power beyond me had governed my directions. From that moment on, I had no more fear about anything. I knew that I was doing the right thing for children; I was making a difference.

Shortly thereafter, the last bell rang for dismissal, and I went to my assigned area on the backside of the school to supervise students leaving the building. About seventy-five percent of the student body walked home, and this evening, it seemed as though every other student spoke or said, "See you tomorrow." When

Nancy came by, she stopped and said, "Mr. Edwards, thank you, I had a good time today. Are we going to square dance tomorrow?" I replied, "No, not tomorrow; but the next day." She came over, hugged my leg and said, "Goodbye. I'll see you tomorrow." Then, she headed for home. I watched her until she was out of sight. I thought to myself, "What a miracle. This child has only vestiges of fingers, but she is proving what can happen if one will encourage a child to learn." In this case, Nancy learned to accept herself as God had made her. Self-esteem building was now real to me.

When I went back into the building to get prepared for checkout for the day, there stood all three fifth-grade teachers, talking about what changes their students had experienced. They asked me about Nancy and this square dancing that all the children were talking about. I smiled and told them that they would have to come to the next class and see for themselves. I continued on toward the front office as they followed, asking one question after the other about square dancing and talking about the way the kids were taking to it. As we approached the front office area, a sixth-grade teacher was talking with a seventh-grade teacher about the same subject. They asked identical questions about square dancing, and I gave the same answers.

I checked out, and as I headed for my car, there stood my three basketball partners. They begged me to play at least one game with them. I was in such good spirits that I agreed to play them the best two-out-of-three games. My team won, and just before I got ready to leave, one of the boys said to me, "Mr. Edwards, we think we are going to like square dancing. Today, we had fun, and we will be ready tomorrow. Please call our group." I promised them that I would.

On the way home, I thought about what a marvelous day it had been! Everything had gone perfectly, and I felt as though the weight of the world was off my shoulders. When I reached home, I was so tired that I could barely get out of the car. But, my-oh-my, was I glad to be there! I got refreshed, prepared my evening meal and, shortly after I ate, laid down across the bed, drifting off into a deep sleep. I slept all night — the best sleep that I had enjoyed in some time. When morning arrived, I was ready, refreshed and hoping for a repeat of the previous day.

19

Square Dancing
Spreads Like Wildfire

I reported for work about twenty minutes early. When I walked into the front office, Mr. Christopher got up from behind his desk, came out to shake my hand and said, "Good morning!" He went on to say that he had received glowing reports from everybody about my square dance classes, and that he was going to come and check me out. I responded that I would welcome his visit and would also teach him how to square dance. After we had a good laugh from that statement, I went on to my class to prepare for the morning.

About twenty minutes later, the first bell rang, notifying students that it was time to go to their homeroom classes. I quickly moved to the door to greet the students as they entered the room. That morning, they were all saying, "Good morning" to me, and I thought to myself, "What a change."

A minute or two later, Nancy arrived — this time running toward me with her hands out to hug me. She hugged my leg while asking, "Are we going to square dance today?" I replied that we weren't, but that I was glad to see her that morning. Then, she was off to class. Throughout the day — every time she saw me — she would ask the same question, "Can I go to P.E. class with you and teach the other children how to square dance?" I would always say, "Yes, but not today." She would ask, "When?", and I would say "Tomorrow."

The next day came, and who did I see ten to fifteen minutes earlier than I would normally see her? Nancy! She came directly to me and said, "Mr. Edwards, today is the day for square dancing, and I am ready." When it came time for her P.E. class, she was among the first students to enter the room. She now wanted to lead the exercises before square dancing. I allowed her to do so, and to my surprise, she was a great leader. Immediately after exercises, we got ready for square dancing; Nancy was the first person on the floor. She and I started things off again, and all of the other students were clapping their hands and cheering "Nancy-Nancy-Nancy." They, too, were having fun. Some of the students were still a little reserved about touching Nancy's hands, but she was no longer ashamed or reserved about touching theirs. When one of her classmates would touch her hands with reservation, Nancy would say "Catch my hands. They won't bite you. Here, catch them." And, she would grab their hands.

When the class period was over, Nancy had been on the floor with at least four other groups for about sixty percent of the time. As I directed the class to get in line for dismissal, Nancy was standing beside me as though she were an instructor. She began telling the students that they were not in line correctly or that she heard too much noise. As some of the students exited the room, I noticed a slight resentment toward Nancy because she was becoming too bossy and getting too much of my attention. She was the last student to leave, repeatedly requesting to stay and help with the next class. I told her that she couldn't and encouraged her to go to her next class. At the end of each P. E. class, she would ask if she could come back the next day to help me with my square dance classes. When I declined her request, she would say, "Well, I tried. I'll see you next time."

At the end of the day, I went outside to assist with dismissal. Almost every student that came by on the way home was now speaking to me or saying, "Goodbye." Shortly afterwards, I went to the front office to check out for the day and observed a number of teachers talking about square dancing and how much the students were beginning to like going to P.E. class. That was certainly refreshing to me; so, I validated their statements by telling them that, yes, the students were having fun. I went on to say that I would like to teach the entire faculty and staff how to square dance. I was surprised when three of them said they thought that that would be wonderful. They added that they were ready, and asked when they could start. I really thought they were putting me on, so I said we could start that next week. They wanted the details, like when and where.

Mr. Christopher walked up and asked what all the chatter was about. One of the teachers spoke up and said, "Mr. Edwards is going to teach us how to square dance." He said that that would be great, and that we should get started right away. He added that the square dance activity had worked wonders with Nancy Johnson, and we all agreed.

As I proceeded to leave the office, I promised that I would hold sessions for them every Tuesday and Thursday from 3:15 to 4:15 p.m. One of the teachers volunteered to be the teacher group leader and would get those who were interested to be there and on time. Then, we left for home. I was overwhelmed by such changes in the attitudes shown by these teachers. I thought that maybe square dancing was now a miracle activity. First, Nancy was out of her shell; then, the other students were having fun; and now, the teachers were seemingly ready to improve our social relations.

20

Finally, In Flight

I was very proud that things were beginning to take shape, and I was having fun! The next day, I showed up for school and there was Nancy; this time before the bell rang for school to start. She wanted to square dance with other classes to show them how to do it. She had become the expert! I didn't allow her to miss her other classes, but she was so enthusiastic that I saw her every day whether it was her time for P.E. or not.

Nancy became so outgoing that she started getting into fights with any student who said anything about her hands. On occasion, I would have to walk her home because she had hit one of the students during the day and that student was waiting for her after school for retaliation. Some students never stopped teasing Nancy about her hands, calling her "Nubbie." And, when they did, they never forgot it because Nancy would hit whoever had made such a statement. I would counsel with her about not allowing what people said to cause her to react to them in a negative manner. And, there were times when I had to discipline her for responding to or causing the problem. That continued for a while, but somewhere near the end of the second quarter during that year, Nancy made the adjustment and was less defensive.

At the beginning of the third quarter, we were cruising. Nancy was managing her behavior, and the students had finally accepted her condition. In addition, much of the apprehension about me was over.

I started an extended-day P.E. program that offered organized free play for students in grades four through seven. The program was from 3:15 p.m. to 4:15 p.m., Monday through Friday. We would take down the tables and move the chairs in the cafeteria for gymnastics and square dancing, and on the outside, we had softball and basketball going concurrently. A number of teachers were attempting to learn square dancing, and students were teaching them! What a beautiful sight — students directing teachers! My immediate role was that of supervisor. On occasion, Mr. Christopher would stop by to observe the activities, especially the square dancing. He would smile and say, "Keep it going." The teacher participation began to draw larger crowds, so I had to offer square dancing every other day in order to effectively supervise the group.

Mr. Thompson, the P.E. Coordinator from the Central Office, as well as a large number of parents, would stop by to see what was creating so much excitement at school. Square dancing became such a popular activity that I had to put on a P.E. program for the PTA (Parent-Teacher Association); we had the largest crowd for a PTA program that I had ever witnessed! I had about a hundred students involved, and the parents were ecstatic. Nancy had fun and was hardly noticed by the crowd. She was not the best square dancer, but she appeared to be the happiest one there. I had never before witnessed anybody make such a drastic change in social development. By the end of the school year, in fact, on the last day of school, Nancy stopped by and said to me, "Mr. Edwards, thank you for helping me. I had a good time. Now, I'm going to be like other little girls. I'm going to learn how to play the piano." She hugged my leg and gave me a letter that read:

Dear Mr. Edwards,

Thank you so much. You are a good P.E. teacher, the best that we have had here at school. Please come back next year.
                                                        Love,
                                                        Nancy

After reading Nancy's letter, I thanked her and told her she had been fun, too. I told her that I wanted her to be like other little girls and when she learned how to play the piano, I wanted her to play me a song. I also told her that I believed in her and that she could do anything that she wanted to and to not let anything stop her from reaching her goals. She looked up at me, smiled and skipped off saying, "Goodbye. You will see." I never thought anymore about that conversation, but I was glad things had gone so well.

During my end-of-year conference with Mr. Christopher, I received a glowing report. When I signed my contract for the next year, he shook my hand and said, "Mr. Edwards, it has been a number of years since I observed a teacher with your abilities. You have really made a difference in the lives of all of us — parents, teachers, and students. I sincerely hope that you will come back next year. You have a bright future in the field of education. Keep up the good work. You are an unusual person." He asked what my plans were for the summer. I thanked him for his kind comments and told him that I had tremendously enjoyed the school year. I also told him that I was planning to attend graduate school that summer and then return for the next school year. He stood up, shook my hand again, hugged me, and said, "Best of luck, and I will see you this Fall."

While leaving Mr. Christopher's office, a number of teachers in the front office began telling me goodbye, to have a great summer and that they would see me next year. I responded warmly and assured them that it was my intent to return. Then, I left the building and headed for my car where eight to ten students were waiting with their hands out wanting me to "give them five." I gave them all "five" by hitting them in their hands. When I got in my car to leave, they were still standing there waving and telling me goodbye, to take care, and they hoped I would come back next year. I left with a great feeling, very proud of the success that had been accomplished. Who would have believed that a school year that started off with such turbulence, would turn out to be so rewarding?

21

What a Difference a Year Makes

I re-entered the University of Montevallo to begin my graduate school program. I worked on a double Masters' degree in Physical Education and in the area of School Administration and Supervision. I was quite busy that summer, so it passed by quickly. I completed twelve hours of graduate credit and had two weeks of vacation before it was time to return to work.

At the beginning of the third week in August, I reported back to Hooper Alexander Elementary School for preplanning. Upon entering the front office, a number of teachers standing there welcomed me with open arms. They were very glad to see me, and I was glad to see them. Mr. Christopher came out of his office to see what all the noise was about, and when he saw me, he came over, shook my hand and said, "I've been talking about you all summer. We are all glad to see you. The parents and students have been asking about you." He introduced me to the new Assistant Principal, Mr. Archie Brown, a middle-aged white man with a very friendly smile. We shook hands, and he said he had heard a lot about my school-wide square dance activities. I was almost speechless by such a warm welcome and the kind words from everyone. I told Mr. Brown that I was glad to meet him and that he would have to join our faculty square dance group. He smiled and said he would wait and see. I assured him that before the year was over, he would be a pro. We all had a big laugh and then broke up and went to our homerooms. I thought about last year's reception and how difficult it had been just to get a "Good morning" from the other staff members and then thought, "What a difference a year had made!"

Shortly thereafter, the bell sounded for everyone to report to the Media Center for our first staff meeting. I could hardly walk down the hall without someone speaking to me. And, when I entered the Media Center, those teachers with whom I hadn't yet spoken seemed to all speak at once, "Mr. Edwards, you are back!" Then, they gave me a round of applause. Mr. Christopher had to call for their attention on two occasions.

After the meeting, many of the teachers and I stayed around and chatted about the summer and our plans for the year. Mr. Christopher stopped on his way out and told me that I had made a lot of people happy. He said that he hoped I realized that I was highly appreciated. I thanked him and moved on to start planning for the year.

Mid-week, the parents and students showed up for registration, and it seemed like every child came by the P.E. office to see me. On the last day for registration, Nancy showed up and came running down the hall to give me a hug. She kept saying, "You're back! You're back! We are going to have fun this year!" She had grown a lot, and she didn't have anything covering her hands. She tried to tell me about everything she had done over the summer and tried to convince me she was taking piano lessons. While I was reluctant to believe her, I encouraged her to do her best and to remember that I was still holding her to her promise of playing me a song. She looked at me and said, "I promise," and then continued registering for school. After she finished registering, she stopped back by my P.E. office to talk about her love for square dancing and said she was glad she would be taking P.E. with me every day instead of every other day like in fifth grade. I assured her that I was glad to see her back and that we would continue our square dancing activities. She wanted to know if she could help me teach everybody how to square dance. I asked her why, and she told me, "It has helped to change my life, and everyone should know how." That was a very touching answer, so I promised that, on occasion, I would let her help. She thanked me and said that now we were going to help everybody. Then, she reminded me that she was learning how to play the piano and had been working all summer trying to learn how to play. I smiled and said, "Don't forget, when you learn how to play, you will have to play me a song."

As she left my office, I couldn't help but marvel at the obvious confidence and determination expressed by Nancy. More than anything else that had happened that week, Nancy's return and her attitude sanctioned why I still wanted to teach.

The official first day of school started the next week, and it seemed as though every parent and student in grades one through seven who came within ten feet of my door had to speak. Some, both parents and students, were hugging me and saying how glad they were to see me back. The few black parents that had known me the year before were pressing forward trying to shake my hand. A number of black parents, new to the school, were standing around trying to get to meet me. There was such a crowd around my door that the new Assistant Principal, Mr. Brown, had to encourage all the students to go to their classes. As they slowly drifted off, Mr. Brown said to me, "You are a celebrity. These people think an awful lot of you." He went on to say that I had won over a lot of people, and he would do anything he could to help me keep things going. I thanked him for stopping by and vowed to help him. We shook hands and were off to a great start.

22

Enjoying Teaching

I resumed all the procedures that had been in operation the year before. Returning students knew just what to expect and new students were easily acclimated to the routine. Nancy continued her social improvement, and square dance became a popular pastime. Occasionally, parents, students, and staff would stop by the cafeteria for after-school P.E. and square dance. Mr. Brown was very active, and we all liked him a lot. He would try almost anything. I looked up one evening, and there was Mr. Brown in the middle of the floor learning to square dance with students and teachers. This turned out to be such an enjoyable activity until it seemed everything in P.E. revolved around where we were going to have square dance. I expanded P.E. classes to include everyday exercises — two laps around the P.E. field or basketball court, basketball, volleyball, kickball, softball, and tinikling (the Philippine bird dance). I would bring the tape player outside when the weather was good, and we would have about five activities going at once. Each day, I would rotate groups to have a balance in their development.

Mr. Brown would help me obtain anything that would improve the P.E. program. I requested bamboo poles for my tinikling dance, and it seemed like I had them in less than a week's time. This dance was easy to teach because the students were ready to learn. The students enjoyed this dance, but not as much as square dancing.

Later that year, we put on another P.E. program for one of the PTA meetings. Mr. Brown and those staff members who had been square dancing agreed to be on the program and to perform. I had about a hundred students involved, and the parents turned out like we were having a national basketball playoff game. Needless to say, it was a total success. The parents loved it, and the students had a great time.

Mr. Christopher was very busy that year with the development of the school system's local professional organization. Periodically, he would stop by my room or I would see him in the cafeteria, and he would say, "I am hearing of the many fine things that you are continuing to do, and I am very proud of you." This would happen about two or three times a month. I would always respond graciously to his words of praise and attribute much of my success to a team effort. While I thought that response was politically correct, I knew deep down within that God, my personal savior, had freed me from many of the social bondages that had plagued me my first six months on the job.

Around Christmas time, the parents and students gave me more gifts than I could imagine. I could hardly get them in my car. Nancy drew me a card that said, *"Merry Christmas Mr. Edwards, you are the best teacher in the whole wide world."* Her gift was the most touching because I knew that it had come from her heart, and perhaps, was the best that she could offer.

We went on to have a great Field Day at the end of the school year. Nancy stopped by my P.E. office on the last day of school to say goodbye for the summer. She assured me she was still working on her music and that she was going to play me a song. Like always, I encouraged her to continue and said I was proud of her. She hugged my leg and said, "I am out of here for the summer."

Shortly after Nancy left, Mr. Brown stopped by to chat a moment and expressed his pride in the very successful year we had just experienced. While we were talking, Mr. Christopher walked in and thanked me for a job well done. Then, he shared that he would not be coming back the next year. However, he said he hoped that I was coming back because I was good for education. I thanked him for all his support during those two years and asked who his replacement would be. He smiled and said it would be Mr. Brown. We hugged each other, and Mr. Brown said he would be greatly dependent on me. To that, I replied that I would be back. We shook hands, and I was off for the summer.

On my way home that evening, I thought what another joyful closure it had been. Everything had gone so well — almost to perfection. I thanked God for having helped me be successful with Nancy and with a number of other people with whom it had been difficult to work.

A few days later, I was back in graduate school at the University of Montevallo. Again, the summer passed by quickly. Graduate school was really fun because it was a break from having children to supervise and parents to worry about. It was during those summer graduate classes that I really got a true sense of what having a responsibility meant.

Then, summer school was over. It was a repeat of the previous summer— two weeks of vacation—but this time, I looked forward to vacation being over because I was anxious to get back to work.

23

Tears of Joy

I reported back for work the third week of August and got the same reception that I had received my second year. Everybody was glad to see me, and everybody was back except Mr. Christopher. Mr. Brown was Principal and Mr. Paul Warner, a black male, was the new Assistant Principal. When he was introduced to the faculty, we gave him a warm reception. I walked over to shake his hand and to personally welcome him. He shook my hand and said that he had heard a lot about me and looked forward to working with me. He was somewhat reserved, yet very professional. For some reason, it appeared that he was going to be a little distant from the staff. While I thought I understood Mr. Warner's "stand-offish" disposition, I didn't want to see it again. I didn't know where he had come from, but I wanted to tell him that our staff had overcome the reason to display that image. But then, I thought it would be better for him to learn that for himself.

The first day of my third year at Hooper Alexander Elementary School was so identical to the year before that I could have re-read the script. Nancy came by with a gift in her hand and yelled, "Mr. Edwards, you are back! Thank God. Here is a little something that I have for you. Take it and set it on your desk." She had two pictures of herself in a frame. She had grown a lot and was presenting herself with increased self-confidence. She told me that she had been working very hard over the summer on her music and that she had a surprise for me. I took her pictures and placed them on my desk. By that time, other students were speaking to me and hugging me so much that I could hardly keep them quiet.

Mr. Warner was walking the halls and stopped by to encourage the students to move on to their classes, but none of them moved. They didn't know Mr. Warner and weren't following his directions. I instructed them to quiet down a bit and then introduced Mr. Warner to them as the new Assistant Principal. I went on to say that I was glad to see them back and that we would talk more later. When I told them that they should go on to their classes, they began to move out slowly. As they left, some were still saying that they were glad to see me back.

That year, my assignment had changed somewhat from having to teach the first two hours and then going out for P.E., to being part Counselor and part P.E. Coordinator. Mr. Brown wanted me to have more time working with all students. This gave me the opportunity to see students from kindergarten through the seventh grade. The Primary teachers loved the idea, and so did the students.

On occasion, Mr. Warner would come out to observe my P.E. classes and would tell me that my classes were well-organized. He didn't care that much about square dancing and never participated with the other staff members. Nevertheless, for me, everything was on automatic. I could blow my whistle, stand up, or wave my hand without saying a word, and the students would obey. Square dancing was still the popular pastime, and all of them were involved to some degree.

Nancy was on track. Things had improved so much that her disability was no longer an issue. She had matured tremendously and competed in any area that was of interest to her. She would find a way, every day, to talk to me about something or another, and putting her off was not easy. She wanted to talk about an array of things — "Why did Mr. Christopher leave?" "What was it like to be a teacher?" "What career should I choose?" "Why was slavery necessary?" "Why was race an issue?" "Why are you not the Principal?" And the list went on and on. Why? What? Where? Who? When? (SMILE!)

A week before Christmas, I got the greatest shock of my young career when Nancy came to school with her music books. She met me in the hall that morning and said, "Mr. Edwards, I am ready to play you a song, so make sure that you give me some time today. I am ready." I promised that I would hear her later that day and knowing Nancy, 'later that day' meant that every time she saw me it would be time to play the song. Finally, somewhere about mid-afternoon, she saw me standing in front of the cafeteria and walked up to me to say, "Mr. Edwards, let's go right now and get this over with." She grabbed me by my shirt and started pulling me into the cafeteria heading toward the piano. I went along with her program, primarily to get it over, because she was not going to quit until I had heard her play a song.

We walked over to the piano; she pulled out the stool, sat down, put up her music and said to me, "Are you ready?" When I told her that I was, she began playing *Silent Night.* I looked at Nancy's hands on the keyboard, and it took great restraint not to cry. I was so amazed that I asked her to play it two or three times because I wanted others to hear and to see this phenomenon that I was witnessing. She drew a crowd, and we started singing as she played. Many students were stunned and were saying to themselves that they couldn't believe their eyes that this girl was playing the piano without all of her fingers. When she completed the song, we gave her a standing ovation. She hugged me and said, "Do you believe me now? I told you I was going to do it. And, I am going to get better." She politely picked up her sheet music from the piano and said, "You haven't seen nothing yet! I'm going to make these hands do things that you won't believe. You just wait and see."

We left the cafeteria, and I directed her back to her class, but she refused to go alone. She wanted me to tell her teacher where she had been. So, I walked her to the classroom and knocked on the door. Ms. Catherine Cook, her music teacher, came over, opened the door and asked Nancy where she had been. I responded, "Ms. Cook, she was with me playing the piano, and you must see this for yourself." Ms. Cook didn't believe me and said, "I have got to see this for myself." She directed Nancy over to the piano and told her to play. Nancy repeated her rendition of *Silent Night* that she had played in the cafeteria. Ms. Cook started applauding Nancy before she had completed playing the song. Then, the students joined in. I left them talking and headed back to my P.E. office. I met Mr. Warner who said he had heard that Nancy had been playing the piano and that he wanted to see that for himself. Well, the news was traveling like wildfire, and Nancy had become a bright star in the eyes of many of her peers.

I was overwhelmed with joy for Nancy because now she was not only square dancing; she was beginning to challenge life for what it had to offer. I couldn't help but think about what she had been like that first time I challenged her to participate in square dancing. Now, she was beyond fearing undertaking anything that she wanted to do, and I thanked God for helping me to help her. Nancy was free and courageous, and I wondered what mission would be next on her agenda.

In a few days, we were out for Christmas, and I received another bundle of gifts. But, the greatest gift I enjoyed that Christmas was Nancy's accomplishment. It was soon over, and I thought no more about it. When we returned to school after the holidays, now and then, someone would mention that Nancy could play the piano, but no one made a big deal about it anymore, and neither did Nancy. Nancy stayed active throughout the remainder of the year trying almost anything that she wanted to do. She played volleyball and kickball and became very knowledgeable about softball and baseball because she would keep score. She was a big help to me doing field activities because she was always willing to assist.

The last two or three days of school — just before her seventh-grade promotion exercise — she brought me a letter that read: *"Mr. Edwards, thank you for being so kind to me. You have helped me so much until I can't thank you enough."* She added that she wished I were going over to the high school with them. Her additional remarks stated that she was going to be like other girls in high school — active in clubs and that she was going to learn how to type and continue to make me proud of her. She closed her letter by writing: *"Thank you, thank you, thank you, forever. Love, Nancy."*

Just before the graduation program on the last day of school, Nancy came by my P.E. office with her mother. She asked if I had read her letter and said not to throw it away because she meant every word. She gave me a gift, hugged me, said, "Thank you," and left the room crying. Her mother and I, for the first time that I could remember, talked about five minutes. She said she could not begin to thank me for what I had done and what it had meant to Nancy. She wished me luck in my career and said she would pray that God would always bless me. As I was about to become emotional due to her overly-kind expressions, other parents walked up to say similar things, so I shook her hand and told her it had been my pleasure and to take care of Nancy.

After the program was over, Nancy came by to hug me again and to say goodbye. She told me that she would be coming back occasionally to see me. This was done very quickly because other students and their parents were doing the same thing.

I was very proud of that class, and especially of Nancy, because we had endured a lot together. That entire class had grown from immaturity to maturity, and Nancy from uncertainty to certainty about herself. She was now fully immersed in life and no longer had to live in isolation. The head and face she once bowed in shame were now elevated with confidence and pride. The hands that were once hidden in shame were now openly in view and her self-esteem, self-acceptance, and social skills ranked beyond the norm. Nancy was no longer asking God why she didn't have fingers like everyone else; she was now thanking God and using what she had. I kept telling myself, over and over, that the students would be just fine. I walked back into my P.E. office, locked the door and let the tears run down my face — tears of joy, mixed with just a little sadness — but, mostly tears of real joy. I looked up and thanked God for helping us to make it because I knew that, together, we had won.

24

The End of the Road as a Teacher

The next week, I continued my summer routine in graduate school. I graduated at the end of the 1974 summer term with a double Master's Degree in Physical Education and School Administration and Supervision. I interviewed for the position of Assistant Principal at Flat Shoals Elementary School, another DeKalb County school, and was offered the position. However, a mix up in the Department of Personnel involving an out-of-state recruit, who had resigned his job and signed a contract with the DeKalb County School System, resulted in both of us being assigned to that position. Because I was already under contract as a teacher, the administration rescinded its offer to me. Consequently, I reported back to Hooper Alexander as a P.E. teacher where Mr. Ray Knight was now Principal. He graciously welcomed me back, and I picked up where I had left off the year before.

In February of 1975, I was promoted to the Assistant Principal's position at DeKalb County's Gresham Park Elementary School. Thus, my career in administration took flight. I stayed at Gresham Park for the remainder of that school year and worked in the Department of Personnel that summer with Miss Alice Ann Hamilton and Ms. Diane Carpenter, employing elementary school classroom teachers. I had a great time working with the people who had employed me. I really wanted to stay and Miss Hamilton, Director of the department, did all she could to keep me. But, she could not get a new position allocated to that department. So, I was reassigned to Hooper Alexander Elementary School as Assistant Principal to Mr. Knight who was still the Principal there.

Supervising those with whom I had once worked as peers proved to be a challenging experience. There were a number of confrontations, but I had the full support of Mr. Knight, and things quickly straightened out. The parents and many of the students were proud that I was back. We had a new P.E. teacher who was encountering a number of problems trying to maintain the quality of the P.E. programs to which the teachers and students had become accustomed. It was hard not to interfere, but I stayed away. Square dance was still popular, and many of the teachers were checking out the square dance record for their individual P.E. time.

As the Assistant Principal, I couldn't give much time to P.E., but it was still in my blood. So, on occasion, I would stop by and square dance a little. But, it was never the same. That special fifth-grade class was gone. Occasionally, a former student would come by and give a brief report, but I never saw Nancy during that year. When that school year ended, I served as Head Administrator for the summer Comprehensive Employment and Training Act (CETA) Program at the Occupational Education Center (OEC) North.

The school system was then highly transitional and social problems were, at times, very difficult to manage. My reputation as a diplomat and communicator had convinced the Superintendent at that time, Dr. James H. Hinson, to utilize my talent wherever he had difficult situations.

At the beginning of the 1977-78 school year, I was reassigned as Assistant Principal to DeKalb County's Leslie J. Steele Elementary School where Mr. Johnny J. Jones was Principal. I stayed there one year. During the summer of 1978, I was promoted to the position of Personnel Administrator in the Department of Personnel. That was the beginning of an entirely different, new career in Central Administration. I was now responsible for employing support staff, assisting in professional staff recruitment, and handling many other general Personnel Department functions.

Once again, I found myself in the position of being the "first black" — this time, the first black Personnel Administrator in the history of the DeKalb County School System. To say the least, that experience was challenging. I was only about twenty-eight years old, but I had the support of Miss Hamilton and her entire staff. She, along with Mr. Bobby Stephens, Mr. Dean Grant, and Ms. Diane Carpenter, made sure that I was thoroughly trained before I was totally released to function without their supervision. In 1983-84, I was promoted to the position of Assistant Director of Personnel for Support Services. I had a staff of nine members to supervise who employed and regulated services for about four to five thousand employees.

25

Again, Nancy Seeks
A Teacher's Touch

In early Spring of 1985, while I was conducting a staff meeting, the Personnel Department's receptionist came to my door and told me that a former student of mine, by the name of Nancy Green, had stopped by unexpectedly, but wanted to stay until she could see me. The name didn't ring a bell at all, but any of my former students who came by to see me were given my full attention. I instructed the receptionist to ask her to please wait; I would be happy to see her as soon as the meeting was over.

The meeting adjourned about five minutes later, and I decided I wanted to go to get this person myself. I walked out to the lobby, and there sat Nancy, now a young woman. When I politely addressed her as Ms. Green, she jumped up and said, "Mr. Edwards, do you remember me? Your shadow from the Hooper days." As she reached out her arms to hug me, I recognized her hands right away. There we were hugging each other and being much louder than we should have been in a public place. There were several other people in the lobby, and they were looking very surprised at the sight of a black man hugging a white woman who was saying that she had been his student. We hadn't seen each other since her seventh-grade graduation, eleven or twelve years before. Returning to some sort of quieter composure, we walked back to my office laughing and talking and trying to quickly catch up on the many years that had passed. She told me that she was married, but was currently separated and in the process of getting a divorce. She added that she had two children. Nancy also indicated that she had not completed high school, which seemed to bother her.

Immediately, I realized that Nancy needed advice, counsel, and direction. While it appeared that she had encountered and conquered a number of life's most difficult challenges, it was also apparent that she was searching for answers that would help relieve some of the pain. Again, I looked her straight in her eyes, somewhat the same way I had when she was in the fifth grade, and I saw those basic things again — uncertainty, stress, fear, and the need of a shoulder to lean on. I responded by saying that the adult world was much different from that of a child, and she said, "Tell me about it!" Tears came up in her eyes, and she started to cry. I thought I would bring a little humor into the situation and said, "Nancy, don't cry, because it really won't help, and if we, as adults, cried every time we had problems, we'd soon be out of tears." She smiled and said, "I know, but that's all you can do sometimes to get a little relief." I agreed with her and admitted there had been a number of times in my life that I had felt like crying, but had realized it really wasn't the solution. Then, she asked if I had any suggestions. I thought a moment before I responded because I realized the marriage problem was perhaps the most complicated, and I didn't want to say anything that would make matters worse. I took her by the hands and said, "Nancy, we had to overcome *this* problem, and today I am proud of you because you have had some success. You are not wearing a towel over your hands, and you are communicating like an adult." She smiled and said, "You're right. Once I got my hands out into the open and you helped me to accept it, I was on my way." She then smiled and said, "You remember me telling you that I was going to learn how to type? Well, I can type forty-five words per minute, and I had to learn that on my own because the teachers wouldn't teach me because I don't have fingers in the right places." I was stunned for the moment by that news, and then I remembered that she had played me a song on the piano, all those years before, at Hooper Alexander Elementary School.

Then, we were back in the "positive zone", talking about success which made it easier for me to address the issues that she had raised. I told her I thought we should take her problems one at a time: her marriage — I asked if she and her husband had gone to counseling. She said they had not and that she felt that the matter was beyond counseling. So, we moved to issue number two, her children: a daughter and a son. I commended her on being a mother and told her that she should be very proud of them. I teased that she should teach them how to square dance. We had a big laugh as we talked about and remembered the old Hooper days. Then, we moved on to issue number three, her high school diploma or, I should say, her failure to stay in school to get one. I strongly encouraged her to go over to DeKalb Technical Institute and to enroll in the General Educational Development (GED) Program. I made sure that she understood that it would become a serious problem for her career if she didn't get a diploma. But also, that from there, other options would open that would make life better for her and her children. I added that college was a possibility because she had great potential.

The entire time I was talking with Nancy, she just stared directly at me and never lost contact with my eyes. It reminded me, so much, of the stare that had occurred that day, years before, when I discovered she only had vestiges of fingers. I had told her then, as I was telling her now, that she could improve her situation if she was willing to try; that it wouldn't be easy, but it would be worth all her efforts.

Then, I began telling her about some of my challenges as an adult and as an administrator for the school system. I informed her that I was a parent with two children and was also a full-time graduate student working on my Doctorate degree, planning to graduate that next May. Then, she broke her silence and said, "Mr. Edwards, that's great! If you are going to get a Doctorate degree, I will promise you that I will get my GED and then go to college somewhere and at least get a Bachelor's degree." We shook hands to seal that commitment. Then, we stood up and hugged each other again, and she said, "I have one last request. When I am through with my GED, will you please help me get a decent job with the school system with benefits?" I promised her that I would do everything within my powers to help her get a good job.

After making that promise, I thought to myself how difficult that might be because most employers didn't encourage people with disabilities to pursue employment with them. But, before she left my office, I decided that introducing her to my immediate supervisors would lay the foundation for a future conversation about employing her in the school system.

Despite the obvious deformity of her hands, she was quite impressive; her appearance was good, and she related very well to others. In addition, she could type about forty-five words a minute. Along with sharing the fact that she was such a success story in my elementary school teaching days, I wanted to make her feel important and build up her self-esteem again by introducing her to other members of the staff. I walked her through the department introducing her first to Miss Hamilton and then to Mr. Bobby Stephens, Ms. Diane Carpenter, Mr. David Francoeur and Mr. Leo Smith. They all warmly greeted her, and she responded very well. Many of our secretaries were quite reserved when it came their time to greet Nancy. When she would extend her hand, a number of them were reluctant and really didn't know how to respond. But, they all passed the test. They shook her hand, and Nancy beamed with joy.

After she had met everyone, we went back to my office to get her jacket in preparation for her to leave. However, before she left, I said to her, "Nancy, the problems you have mentioned are not the worst things that could happen to a person. They are life experiences, and you must learn to cope with life's challenges. So, I'm requesting that you do the following things: (1) pray; (2) let God help you with your problems; (3) attend your church regularly; (4) talk with your mother, on occasion, about life's trials; (5) keep the job you have until you complete your GED Program; (6) take care of your children; and (7) stay in touch with me, and keep me posted as to how you are progressing."

Nancy thanked me for taking the time to talk with her and for introducing her to the other people in the department. She went on to say that she was glad to know that I had not changed and that she wished me luck in getting my Doctorate degree. She hugged me and said she would be back to see me sooner than I might think. I responded by saying that I was proud of her and would be highly disappointed if she did not follow my suggestions. She laughed and said, "Mr. Edwards, have I ever broken my promise? If I say I'm going to do it, you can look for it." We said goodbye, and she was on her way.

Later that day, I stopped by to visit a number of the individuals to whom I had introduced Nancy; primarily to hear their comments. They all spoke of her self-confidence and pleasant disposition and how well she had adjusted to her disability. Needless to say, I was very proud to hear such positive remarks because I knew that I would need them if Nancy came back looking for employment. Miss Hamilton and Mr. Stephens said they were impressed with Nancy and would help me in any way they could to find employment for her if she came back. But, they also warned me it would not be easy to locate a job for her because of her disability. I thanked them for their support and went on to say how good it would be for our department's record to reflect that we employed disabled individuals whenever possible. That idea was well-received, and from that day on, we actively looked for persons with disabilities to employ.

I went back to my regular routine still thinking, now and then, how great it had been to see Nancy again. I continued my dreadful evenings and weekends working to complete my Doctorate degree. The grueling challenge of this experience soon overshadowed the memory of Nancy having stopped by to see me.

26

Employing Nancy

A year later, the first of August 1986, Nancy called and left her number for me to call her. When I returned the call and she realized I was on the phone, she said, "Mr. Edwards, are you a doctor yet?" I said, "No, but I am getting close." Then she said, "Guess what? I have completed my GED Program, and I am going to DeKalb College." She went on to say that everything else was working out — not the best — but better.

Then, she said she needed a job. So, we began talking about her coming in for an interview with one of the Personnel Administrators. A few days later, she came in for the interview with Mr. Francoeur who was responsible for employing clerical staff. She was also scheduled (as were all clerical applicants) to take a test to assess her clerical skills. She went back to take the typing part of the test, and all the secretaries who knew she was taking the test gathered in that area to witness Nancy's typing. We were all surprised! Nancy did very well on the typing test. She was really amazing, and I was very proud. The same Nancy who had amused me as a seventh-grade student playing the piano, now had amazed me by being able to type with only vestiges of fingers on both hands. After completing the other parts of the clerical test, she was assessed as a viable candidate for employment. Trying to place her would be another matter. Who could we get to give Nancy a chance? I had obtained commitments from Miss Hamilton and Mr. Stephens to assist Mr. Francoeur in locating a position for her. Since Mr. Francoeur worked on my staff, we devoted the necessary time and energy trying to secure a position for her.

Finally, on August 12, 1986, we received commitment from Mr. Mack Ivey, in our Plant Services Department, who agreed to give Nancy a chance. She was employed as a Data Entry Specialist, and I don't know who was happiest — Nancy, myself, or Dave Francoeur. We wished her the best, and she promised to do her best. After she completed her employment forms, she couldn't stop thanking us enough. She kept saying that we would never be sorry for helping her. Then, she was off to the job, and I returned to my stressful assignment, working full-time and being on the down side of completing my Doctorate degree.

Now and then I would hear through Mr. Francoeur that Nancy was doing a good job. I received a card from her saying that she loved her job and thanking me for my help. I called her job, and we spoke briefly. She was very happy to hear from me and said that she had met a very nice man that she was getting serious about. We didn't discuss any other details relative to that matter, so, basically, that was about all I knew about this new man that she had discovered.

In late April of 1987, our Personnel Office received Nancy's annual evaluation, which was very good, along with a letter of resignation stating that she was going to relocate to Florida. She gave a two-week notice; her last day of work was May 14, 1987. That was really a busy time for both of us. Nancy was preparing to leave for Florida, and I was graduating from Clark Atlanta University on that same day. We missed saying goodbye to each other. But, Nancy left a note saying 'Thanks'; that she wished me the best and that she would get back in touch when she got things settled. That was the end of my knowledge of the whereabouts of Nancy Green.

On occasion, I would think about Nancy because she was a real highlight and success story in my early teaching career. I didn't know where she was, but I knew that wherever she was, she was equipped with confidence, courage and pride, and would survive .... and that gave me comfort. When I closed my thoughts of Nancy Green, I said to myself, "I truly helped all that I could, and I believe that I really made a difference in her life."

27

The Reunion

In recounting this story to Ms. Sally Jessy Raphael, I acknowledged that, in retrospect, perhaps this experience was one of my greatest professional accomplishments.

I told Ms. Raphael about my challenging Nancy to the point where she was forced to show her hands and about the humiliation she encountered from other students. I emphasized the fact that I had partnered with Nancy, holding her hands, to demonstrate to the other students that accepting differences was the right thing to do. Perhaps, that had been the first time that someone, outside Nancy's family, had touched her hands and had not rejected her. I'm sure that that action helped her to better accept her disability and gave birth to her increasing her self-acceptance and self-esteem. In addition, the experience helped all the students mature a little.

Ms. Raphael asked when I had last seen or heard from Nancy. I said that I didn't remember exactly, but if I had to guess, I'd have to say about a decade or more, earlier.

Her next question was, "Do you know where she lives?" I responded that maybe she was living in the metro Atlanta area, but I really had no idea.

Ms. Raphael commented that I was highly expressive and communicated exceptionally well— according to her, much different than a number of persons with whom she had already spoken. She said it had been great talking with me and that it was a wonderful story. She had decided to fly Nancy and me to New York to be on her show. She also told me that if Nancy tried to contact me to tell me she was going to be on the show and to request that I go with her, to decline. I was not to give her any information about our conversation and was not to let her know, in any way, that I was going to be on the show. It was to be a big surprise to Nancy.

When Ms. Raphael officially asked if I would come, I said, "Yes." I added, "I am touched, and I would love to be on your show." She gave me telephone numbers for two of her staff members, Joan Petrocelli and Debbie. She said one of them would call me with details and travel arrangements. She said that she was looking forward to meeting me. I thanked her for calling, and we said goodbye.

After my conversation with Sally Jessy Raphael, I was overwhelmed with emotion. How could this be true? I had never imagined or even thought about something like this taking place. I sat there for a moment, stunned over the phone call. I thanked God for having helped me to do the right thing for Nancy - at that moment in her life - and reflected on what could have happened.

Then, there were tears — tears of joy and thanks. I thought for a while about what Nancy's childhood name had been, and a few minutes later, it came to me ..... Nancy Johnson. I also remembered that I had last known Nancy as Nancy Green when I employed her as a Data Entry Specialist. The last name 'Miller' still puzzled me somewhat, but Ms. Raphael had too much information about my past for this not to be the right Nancy from grade school, all those years ago.

After hanging up from talking with Ms. Raphael, I immediately called my wife, Cynthia, and shared the news. We both grew more excited by the moment as we discussed the possible trip to New York City. My whole life began changing as I thought about and relived that entire experience. My spirit was filled with humility and, at times, literally, all I could do was cry. So, I stayed away from people as much as I could the first day or two until I could control my emotions.

On Thursday, September 19, 1996, around mid-morning, Joan Petrocelli called with details of my travel arrangements. We were scheduled to tape the live program on Tuesday, September 24 (my wife's birthday). While this trip required only an overnight stay for a one-day activity, Cynthia and I left on that Saturday, September 21, to visit and enjoy New York City for a few days before the taping.

We arrived in New York that Saturday evening; a limousine met us at the airport to take us to the hotel where we had a reservation. Without my knowledge, Nancy arrived in New York City on Monday, September 23; she had a reservation at a hotel quite a distance from where we were staying. It would have taken another miracle for us to run into each other — besides, she wasn't expecting me to be there.

On the morning of September 24th, we were scheduled to check out of the hotel and be in the limousine by 7:45 a.m. in order to be at the Sally Jessy Raphael Studio by 8:00 a.m. As we were standing in front of the hotel, people were asking who we were. We were taking pictures and having fun with another couple riding with us who were also scheduled to be on the show.

By that time, I was feeling excited as well as uncertain. I was hoping that this Nancy was the right Nancy so that none of us would be embarrassed. While I was trying to deal with this matter internally, I was pretending to be "cool, calm, and collected."

Cynthia and I settled ourselves in the limousine without first making sure that our luggage was with us. When we arrived at the studio and the driver unloaded the luggage, we were quite surprised when ours wasn't there. More pressure — where is our luggage and will we ever find it? Time would not allow me to go back and look for it, so Cynthia took a cab back to the hotel to find the missing luggage. Ms. Raphael's staff of producers and counselors took the other guests and me to an isolated room where we would not come in contact with Nancy and the other guests scheduled for the show.

Now, I had three major concerns: Would Cynthia find our luggage and get back in time for the taping of the show? Was this Nancy the same Nancy I had taught all those years ago in grade school? How would I respond to this extraordinary reunion on national television?

Shortly after we were settled in the holding room, the producers and counselors began interviewing us, styling our hair, and putting on camera make-up. There were about five or six of us, and we were all "first timers." A producer interviewed me first, which took about three to five minutes to be considered ready for the show.

I was glad the room was on the front of the studio because I could watch through the window for Cynthia. We had about a two-hour wait before the show started, and I spent the next half-hour worrying about Cynthia and our luggage. I must have counted twenty cabs before one finally stopped in front of the studio, and the driver opened the door for Cynthia to step out. Half the worry was over. And, when the driver took our luggage out of the trunk, the other half was over. I very quietly, to myself, thanked God for helping us to get our luggage back. One of the staff members brought Cynthia to our room, and one of my problems was behind me.

Several minutes later, I was scheduled for make-up. Once that was over, it was time to head for the stage. The producers lined us up, with me at the front of the line, and led us down a long hallway which, at times, seemed to be underground. We went to another room where we were instructed on how to use the microphone system and when to walk on stage. I walked behind the stage and stood behind the curtain. About two minutes later, Ms. Raphael came by and introduced herself. She said, "Lonnie Edwards, I have heard so much about you from my staff. You are a wonderful person, and I am proud to have you on my show." I graciously thanked her, and she walked out on the stage.

The cameraman began adjusting the cameras to focus directly on me, and one of the producers was giving me last-minute instructions. I could see what was taking place on the stage and in the audience. Ms. Raphael began introducing the show and giving a brief overview of her first guests. She explained to the audience that her first guest, Nancy, wanted to thank her gym teacher, Lonnie Edwards, who was "missing in action," and that Nancy was trying to find him to say "thanks" for helping her to shine when she was in the fourth or fifth grade. She went on to say that Nancy had been handicapped from birth — born basically without fingers on either hand. Then, she requested that Nancy come out to meet the audience and to visit with her. When Nancy walked out on stage, I immediately looked for her hands, and when she extended her hand to Ms. Raphael, I was certain that she was the right Nancy. Another worry over!

As she told our story, I could not hold back my tears. While Ms. Raphael questioned Nancy about me and her grade-school experience, I could not contain my emotions, and when Nancy raised up her hands, I thought I would burst inside from trying not to cry. I couldn't help but think about the hands that she had once hidden from her schoolteachers and classmates. Now, she was raising them with pride to expose them on national television and to express her thanks to me for helping her to overcome them. A feeling of humility came over me that I will never be able to describe, especially when she read a poem that she had written about me. (Placed in the front of the book.) She thanked me and asked the studio audience and everyone watching at home that if they knew my whereabouts, to please let her know. It was just remarkable!

Nancy said, "*Mr. Edwards, wherever you're at. I just want to tell you thank you for the great job that you did. No matter whatever happens to you or whatever happens to me, the legacy that you leave behind will be a whole system of students ... because you did a job! You weren't just a teacher, a Vice Principal, and now an administrator of a school system, you were actually all of our friend. And, I want to tell you thank you, and I will always be there in your heart, if not, in spirit and soul also.*"

As I stood there looking at Nancy and listening to her, I was overwhelmed with humility, realizing that I was experiencing the ultimate thanks, a teacher's dream. I was wishing that I could be granted just five minutes to cry because nothing in my whole life had created such emotions. I was truly touched. Ms. Raphael made the statement, "If anyone out there knows where Mr. Edwards is, please let me know." And, as I had been instructed, I said, "I know where he is," and walked from behind the stage with a bouquet of flowers for Nancy.

When Nancy looked and saw me, we ran toward each other and embraced with tears just flowing down our faces. What a moment! I hadn't seen or heard from Nancy for almost ten years. What a surprise! I could hardly compose myself for the three- to five-minute interview that we had with Ms. Raphael. However, I did give a few statements about myself and our historic and dramatic association.

I cannot begin to describe the feeling that I experienced during that moment of reuniting with Nancy. It was surreal. It might fit well in the category of a dream versus reality. You believe it's there, but you are not sure. You see it and wonder how it could be. Then, I surrendered and acknowledged the miraculous acts of God; I felt that we were living proof that something divine had taken place.

Nancy was expressing thanks for something that had occurred about twenty-five years earlier. Although I had helped her to get a job a decade earlier, we had not talked, at any time, about anything near the subject of my having made a difference in her life. As an educator, I have always pulled for each child and have experienced the expression of thanks from a number of young people who I have assisted along the way. But, I dare say that very, very few of us have gone to the extent that Nancy did, to say thanks.

I found out that Nancy had gone back to school and completed an Associate and two Bachelor degrees. She was writing, typing and using the computer as well as, if not better than, most. She was playing the piano for leisure (after taking lessons for ten years) and was President of her homeowners association. In addition, she and her husband, Daniel Miller, had a blended family of five children. To think that of the many individuals and teachers Nancy had encountered in her life, she thought way back to the fifth grade and selected me as the spark that had set her to flame, was overwhelming.

As we left the stage heading to the guest room, I was remembering Nancy more as a child than as an adult. So, we began our conversational journey talking about things that had happened twenty-five years before and of people I had forgotten.

We later went to lunch at one of the nearby restaurants accompanied by my wife, Cynthia, and several other people who also had been guests on the show. After lunch, we returned to the studio where we were scheduled to catch the limousine and depart for the airport.

On our way to the airport, we had many laughs, but the most memorable was when I said to Nancy, "Teachers everywhere better take note because they will never know where a fifth-grader will take them. Look at me, in New York City, in a limousine, after being on a national television show, Sally Jessy Raphael, with a student I taught how to square dance in a fifth grade P.E. class twenty-five years ago." Nancy replied, "Teachers had better be careful about what they say and do, because it could come back to haunt them, and even more, if it is negative." And, with that statement, I fell victim to the after-the-fact syndrome and thought about how ashamed I would have been had the story been different.

28

Returning Home

During the flight back home to Atlanta, Cynthia and I discussed the reunion with Nancy and everything that we had experienced over the weekend. She had no idea that I was also thinking about another surprise that I had pending.

At Cynthia's suggestion, we decided to make the weekend in New York City her birthday present. Although I canceled everything else that I had planned, I kept the arrangements for her best friend, Sylvia Anderson, to fly in from Chicago, Illinois. While we were in New York City, I had to steal time away from Cynthia to make phone calls to friends in Atlanta, confirming my revised birthday plans for her. My best friend, Earnest Killum, was to pick Sylvia up from the airport and have her at our home waiting for us.

When we arrived home, Killum was there under the pretense of giving us our mail that he had kept for us while we were out of town. Once we were inside, Sylvia came out of one of our rooms with a huge bow and ribbon tied around herself. Cynthia was elated! So was I; I pulled off a big surprise!

Killum and I talked for a while. He wanted to know all about the New York City experience, and I wanted to share it. After he left, I said, "Good night" to Sylvia and encouraged Cynthia to stay longer so they could begin enjoying their time together.

Upstairs, I unpacked, showered and put on my pajamas. But, before I climbed into bed, I knelt down to thank God for all of His blessings and for the success of the trip. Most of all, I asked for His continual guidance in my every endeavor as I try to contribute to making this world a better place.

In the quiet time that I had by myself before drifting off to sleep, I thought about the importance of every interaction that we, as human beings, have with each other. I thought especially about *a teacher's touch* ... just look at what happened with Nancy.

The end.

Recommendations
on
How to Provide
"A Teacher's Touch"

The following recommendations are designed to help teachers add that special touch to a student's life:

(A.)   Always be kind and loving to children; it is never too soon to demonstrate these qualities.

(B.)   Always remember that the child you are teaching today has a great chance of being an adult tomorrow.

(C.)   Always be careful of what you say to a child because it will have a lasting impression on his/her life.

(D.)   Always remember that maybe, just maybe, one of your students might expose your relationship with him/her on national television. Nancy did. How would you want your story to be told twenty-five years later?

(E.)   Teach them all; counsel them all; coach them all, and encourage them all.

E p i l o g u e

As I close A TEACHER'S TOUCH, I would like to provide an update on what has happened to Nancy and me since our appearance on the Sally Jessy Raphael Show.

The Atlanta Journal-Constitution published a three-quarter-page article on our story called "The Power of Kindness." In addition, a number of other local newspapers and magazines have written their accounts of the story. I have received numerous telephone calls and letters from around the United States from people who saw the Sally Jessy Raphael Show and/or read one of the articles and wanted me to know the impact it made on their lives. I have made a number of speeches for school systems, churches, businesses, state and local organizations, banquets and clubs, etc. The Sally Jessy Raphael Show film clip has been shown to various administrative staffs and faculties for motivation and inspiration.

Nancy and I are in constant contact. She and her husband, Dan, have visited with Cynthia and me on several occasions. Our visits have included attending church together, lunches, dinners, tours, and an Atlanta Braves baseball game, along with joint speaking engagements. Cynthia and I visited Nancy's mother, Ms. Betty Johnson, in Florida and videotaped her thoughts on Nancy as a child as well as our teacher/student interaction.

Together, Nancy and I have appeared on the TBN Network giving a live testimony on the "Earl Paulk Ministries" telecast from the Cathedral of the Holy Spirit in Decatur, Georgia where Cynthia and I worship. Nancy and I were given a book, One Blood, by Bishop Earl Paulk and acknowledged by him as the image of this story.

As a result of the exposure of this story, as well as my ongoing efforts to mentor youth, I have received the following special recognitions:
- a proclamation for Outstanding Service to Education, the Community, and Mankind, signed by Governor Zell Miller, State of Georgia
- one of 11 Community Service Awards presented in 2001 by WXIA-TV, Channel 11 in Atlanta, Georgia
- the 2000 Georgia Legislative Black Caucus Excellence in Education Award

- an award for Outstanding Service and Contribution to Education, by the DeKalb County Board of Education

The DeKalb Board of Education honored Nancy and me with a reception in the Williamson Board Room. A reception was also held for us at Hooper Alexander Elementary School where Nancy and I first became acquainted as teacher and student.

Nancy and I have served as speakers for an annual Teacher-of-the-Year function for two or three hundred teachers, as well as at a quarterly extravaganza meeting for Destiny Telecommunications, Inc. Individually, I have accepted many speaking engagements in the Metro-Atlanta area, as well as in other cities, on many topics, especially those centered on *Human Relations* and *Race Relations*.

We have also organized the **EDWARDS-MILLER FOUNDATION FOR PHYSICAL DISABILITIES, INC.** as a non-profit organization under the IRS Section 501(c)(3) code. The purpose of the foundation is to provide post-secondary scholarships for students, like the other Nancys of the world (physically or mentally challenged), who express a desire and have the ability to obtain a college education, including technical training at a two-year institute.

It is our hope that this foundation will encourage all students to believe that opportunities and a better way of life are possible.

We solicit your support — both financial and in-kind — in this mission because we truly believe and have demonstrated that together we can make a difference.

"You can help us to help others."

THE EDWARDS-MILLER FOUNDATION
FOR PHYSICAL DISABILITIES, INC.
P.O. Box 360741
Decatur, Georgia 30036-0741
770-879-9772 (Telephone) 770-413-2444 (Fax)

edwards_miller@msn.com (e-mail)
www.edwards-miller.org (website)

Your donation is tax deductible.

THANK YOU!

A Teacher's Inspiring Legacy

Nancy Johnson Miller beams as she reminisces with her former teacher, Dr. Lonnie J. Edwards, Sr.

Responding to the Sally Jessy Raphael Show's search for people who wanted to thank someone on national television for changing their life, Nancy wrote about Lonnie.

Nancy was born with multiple physical challenges. She has a severe neurological disorder, resulting in her being epileptic; she also has only small vestiges of fingers, mostly little "nubs." Because of this, while in school, she kept her hands hidden from teachers and students at all times. (One of her hands is shown on the front cover of this book.)

In 1971, when Nancy was in the fifth grade, she met Lonnie Edwards. He was a first-year Physical Education teacher at her school. According to Mrs. Miller, Dr. Edwards was instrumental in her accepting her physical disabilities and in being confident in using and/or developing the talents that God **did** give her. Through their interactions, Nancy gained more self-confidence and decided that she wanted to be "like the other little girls." With a made up mind and a teacher's support, she did just that ... and more!